The
Independent
Walker's Guide
to
Ireland

By the same author

The Independent Walker's Guide to France
The Independent Walker's Guide to Great Britain
The Independent Walker's Guide to Italy

The
Independent
Walker's Guide
to
Ireland

by Frank Booth

35 Memorable Walks
in Ireland's Green Countryside

INTERLINK BOOKS
NEW YORK

First published in 1999 by

INTERLINK BOOKS
An imprint of Interlink Publishing Group, Inc.
99 Seventh Avenue • Brooklyn, New York 11215 and
46 Crosby Street • Northampton, Massachusetts 01060

Library of Congress Cataloging-in-Publication Data

Booth, Frank W., 1951-
    The independent walker's guide to Ireland : 35 memorable
walks in Ireland's green countryside / by Frank Booth.
        p. cm.
    ISBN 1-56656-288-0
    1. Ireland—Guidebooks. 2. Walking—Ireland—Guidebooks.
3. Landscape—Ireland—Guidebooks. 4. Natural areas—Ireland—
Guidebooks.   I. Title.
DA980.B67 1999
914.1504'824—dc21   99-18564
                                                                 CIP

Printed and bound in Canada
10 9 8 7 6 5 4 3 2 1

Contents

Contents

Part Two: 35 Great Walks

Introduction

Although this is a walkers' guide, it is also about escaping and avoiding the DROPS. The DROPS are not a communicable disease. They are something far more insidious: the highly-feared DREADED OTHER PEOPLE who are always in your way, going where you want to go when you want to go. You have seen them everywhere—in long lines at the bank, at the supermarket with bounteous baskets standing six deep in front of you, and in disabled vehicles blocking your path during interminable rush-hour traffic. Great multitudes of DROPS are waiting for you in Ireland.

Seldom will you see a single DROP (perhaps this word can only be used in the plural; a single individual may not qualify for DROPhood). They tend to cluster in large numbers around people who are trying to avoid them. Like stampeding cattle, they destroy everything in their path. International publications have been reporting the results of their rampaging for years: as *Newsweek* put it long ago in July 1992, "These days it is tough to find a vacation spot that doesn't in some way resemble a shopping mall, a garbage dump, or a traffic jam." Even with this book in hand, you will not always be able to completely avoid the DROPS, but you will have a strategy to retain your independence and sanity. For example, if you are sojourning in Dublin, you will want to visit the many great tourist attractions in the city center. Unfortunately, solitude is not to be found, and you will be huddled shoulder to shoulder with numerous DROPS. When you tire of the multitudes, take the thirty minute rail ride to small-town Howth at the end of a peninsula about ten miles north of downtown Dublin; relax at a waterfront restaurant while enjoying the catch of the day which has been trawled from the sea only hours ago; and revel in a spectacular six-mile cliff walk along the troubled waters of the Dublin Bay. You will see none of the DROPS whose elbows you encountered while being jostled about the tourist's Dublin. You can repeat this scenario at many of the most renowned tourist sites in Ireland. You will see the "must-sees," but you will also get way off the beaten path for a glimpse of the *real*

Ireland that is known only to the independent walker.

This book shows you how to walk between and around sites that are endlessly written about in ordinary guides. The trails described in this book will take you to many of Ireland's most famous monuments and also to a variety of lesser known but equally interesting areas. The one or two hours on foot from tourist centers is a world away from the ordinary tourist's view of Ireland. You will enter another dimension (as Rod Serling was fond of saying), and go one step (actually a lot of steps) beyond into the outer limits of an ordinary tour of Ireland. You will see the Irish going about their daily lives on farms, in villages, and along roads too remote to appear on most maps. Local cows, horses, sheep, chicken, and dogs will often be present to greet you. *The Independent Walker's Guide to Ireland* is simply the most versatile, useful, and exciting guide available to this unique island nation. Explore Ireland as a traveler not a tourist, and truly see all of Ireland through the backdoor.

This book is organized into two sections. The first part, Hitting the Trail, provides general information on travel to Ireland and what to expect when you arrive; from how to use public transportation and driving tips to information about hotels and restaurants. And of course it also supplies you with all the information you need to become a successful hiker in Ireland. The second section contains practical information about 35 walks, including distance, time duration, a general description of the trail and a description of local sights. Each walk description also has an accompanying set of trail notes and maps which will alert you to possible problems and confusion along the route and help you plot your course through undiscovered Ireland.

Walking as Opposed to Other Forms of Travel

Why not rent a car or take a train or a bus or even pedal a bicycle? Why walk? There are faster ways of getting around, and if you go faster, you can see more. I understand this mentality and have been on some breathtaking auto tours of Europe, hurtling down expressways from sight to sight at one hundred miles per hour while high-powered German sedans pass at warp speed. If this will be the extent of your vacation, driving quickly between famous sites, stay home, rent a travel video about Ireland, and save money.

Although I recommend travel by car, you should also take the time for frequent walks. When you walk, you create unique memories, avoid the DROPS, and seldom see any mechanized form of transportation. All of these are luxuries afforded to few 21st century travelers.

Trains and buses in Ireland are generally very good, and you will want to use these modes of transportation as an aid to your walking. However, I would not recommend spending valuable vacation time riding around on crowded public transportation, particularly during the summer months when the DROPS assemble en masse. When you take a train or bus, you often miss the most important part of your trip—the trail or what lies between your destinations. There are no surprises on public transportation, and you will probably have numerous DROPS and dirty windows separating you from what you came to see: Ireland.

Some people extol the virtues of bicycling in Europe. Yes, you will get some exercise, and you will see some interesting monuments. You will not, however, get far off the beaten path; bicycles go where cars go—where everyone else goes. The roads that cyclists pedal are less frequented by motorized vehicles but by no means untraveled. Although traffic in Ireland is generally at a snail's pace, the roads are narrow—barely wide enough for two cars—not wide enough for two cars and a bicycle. Do not count on drivers watching out for you; you are definitely on your own. Furthermore, European cars are notorious for their choking emissions and high-decibel noise. On a trail, you will encounter none of these difficulties.

The Independent Walker

This book is designed to help you, an independent traveler, plan a walking tour of Ireland. There is no single way of walking in Ireland, and whether you are relying on your thumb for locomotion and sleeping in an army-surplus pup tent or leasing a Mercedes to shuttle yourself between multi-starred luxury hotels, you will find this book to be worth more than you paid for it.

All of the walks have been selected based on the following criteria: the walk itself is of great visual delight; the trail is near a noteworthy tourist site or in an area of great natural beauty; there is easy access to public transportation. Another unique feature of this book is that almost all of the walks are linear; you will not find yourself walking around in circles (that is, getting nowhere). Linear walks are interesting throughout their entire length; whereas circular walks, which you will find in other walking guides, usually include a less-than-attractive or repetitious return to the starting point. Linear walks also impart a feeling of accomplishment in having arrived at a town or city in the traditional way of our ancestors, on foot. At Dublin, for example, you will trek the final few miles along the eighteenth-century Royal Canal which links Dublin with the River Shannon about ninety miles away, experiencing Ireland's capital city as a Dubliner rather than a tourist. Starting from the far reaches of exurbia, you will ramble through the good, bad, and ugly that great cities conceal from all but the most cognizant travelers. Along the way, you will stride beneath still-functioning, eighteenth-century bridges; be dazzled by frequent stands of wild flowers along the often heavily treed banks; spy rabbits that appear briefly before scurrying back into the bushes; and savor the suavely sophisticated swans that float regally along the canal. You will also witness foreboding factories and warehouses, uninvitingly encased in voluminous reels of razor wire that rise regularly from the boundaries of the canal. At walk's end you will enter Dublin's opulent city center, completing a walk of many contrasts. No other guidebook will take you on a walk like this, into the heart of the real Dublin through the real back door. Similar experiences await you throughout Ireland. You can use a car and public transportation or, if you do not rent a car, use only public transportation to reach starting and ending points. Specific directions are included in the final section for each walk.

In order to plan a remarkable tour of Ireland, consult the map on page 6, and look at the suggested itineraries listed below. For travelers with time to burn, there is a comprehensive itinerary, the Grand Tour, which combines all of the greatest sites with a collection of Ireland's finest walks. The Grand Tour is peerless as a vehicle for an in-depth discovery of Ireland.

There are also four regional itineraries: Dublin and Vicinity, Republic of Ireland: South of Dublin, Republic of Ireland: North of Dublin/ Northern Ireland, and Republic of Ireland: The West from Shannon Airport. Another unique feature of this book is the inclusion of nine thematic tours: Captivating Coasts and Beaches; Inland Waterways; Cathedrals, Churches, and Abbeys; Obscure Villages; High Hills; Verdant Forests; Isolated Islands; The Must-See Itinerary: All the Great Sights; and Author's Favorite Walks.

Although there is a remarkable diversity of tours available to select from, do not consider this to be a strait-jacket. Feel free to construct your own itinerary or combine two or more of the suggested itineraries. In order to determine which particular walks are most attractive for you, inspect the Walks-at-a-Glance section on pages 20-40, which provides capsule summaries of each adventure.

Itineraries

The following diverse itineraries are suggested, but feel free to construct your own via consultation with the maps and walk summaries.

The Grand Tour

For the finest tour available in all of Ireland, complete all of the walks in the order presented (1-35). An ambitious, fast-driving traveler could do them all in about six weeks with a few days left over for a stay in Dublin. For a less frenetic tour, budget about seven or eight weeks.

This itinerary is given in its most compressed form. If you are not on a tight schedule, feel free to intersperse your walks with free days to explore each region in more depth or simply relax. Also, on one-night stops you may not arrive in time to make a required public transportation rendezvous, necessitating an extra day in town; or you may not feel

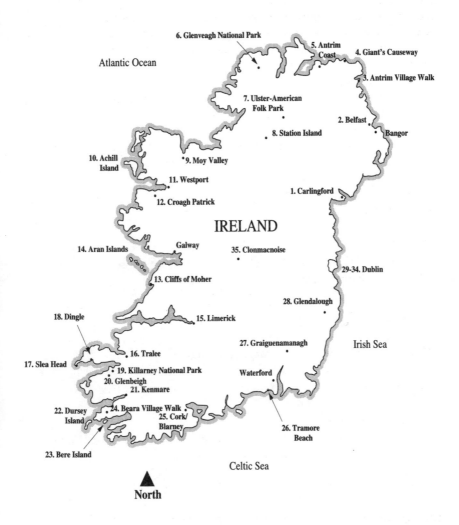

Atlantic Ocean

6. Glenveagh National Park

5. Antrim Coast

4. Giant's Causeway

3. Antrim Village Walk

7. Ulster-American Folk Park

2. Belfast

Bangor

8. Station Island

10. Achill Island

9. Moy Valley

11. Westport

12. Croagh Patrick

1. Carlingford

IRELAND

14. Aran Islands

Galway

35. Clonmacnoise

29-34. Dublin

13. Cliffs of Moher

28. Glendalough

18. Dingle

15. Limerick

27. Graiguenamanagh

Irish Sea

16. Tralee

17. Slea Head

19. Killarney National Park

Waterford

20. Glenbeigh

21. Kenmare

22. Dursey Island

24. Beara Village Walk

25. Cork/ Blarney

26. Tramore Beach

23. Bere Island

Celtic Sea

North

Itineraries Map

like getting out of your car and going immediately on a walk. Be judicious with available time, and do not push yourself too hard. Remember, you are on vacation. On the other hand, it usually is possible for tireless travelers to adhere to the suggested itineraries and enjoy the fast-paced succession of sites and walks. The suggested travel routes are simply the fastest (although the fastest road in Ireland is a relative concept and would probably be the slowest road anywhere else) or most direct. Please ignore them, if you have the time, and create a more interesting route along Ireland's many beautiful secondary roads. These itineraries, which take you to a variety of off-the-beaten-path locations are sometimes more difficult via public transportation and may involve convoluted routing in order to reach some destinations. For the patient traveler, however, it is possible to arrive at almost all of the destinations, and I have included whether it is possible to reach a destination by train or if a train/bus combination is required. You can get detailed information on connections at most train stations, or you can consult *Let's Go: Ireland* for reliable public transportation information. Finally, the suggestions about where to stay can easily be altered to suit your needs; however, they are generally the most attractive alternative in a given area. I have included some specific lodging recommendations, but the tourist office, a quick ride around town or a comprehensive guidebook that specializes in lodging will provide you with a more in-depth overview of the local lodging scene. Rooms are seldom difficult to find in Ireland, especially if you are in a car. However, if you are relying on public transportation, you may wish to consult a comprehensive guidebook and reserve hotel or B&B rooms in advance, particularly during crowded summer months.

Night 1: Carlingford (Walk 1)

From Dublin's Airport take N1 north to R 173 just past Dundalk, which takes you circuitously into Carlingford (about 65 miles/105 kilometers); or you may take a train from Dublin to Dundalk and then a bus to Carlingford. There are several B&Bs in Carlingford but I found the Granvue House (tel. 042-75109) located on the shore of Carlingford Lough just up the road in tiny Omeath to be quite commodious. You could also pass the night in larger Dundalk if the lodging situation appears crowded. Complete Walk 1 between Carlingford and Omeath in the afternoon before you are completely overcome by jet lag.

If your flight arrives later in the day you may need to schedule an extra day here.

Nights 2 and 3: Belfast/Bangor (Walk 2)

From Carlingford, rejoin R173, which becomes B79 until you reach Newry and continue North along A1 which goes directly to Belfast (62 miles/100 kilometers). If you prefer to sojourn in smaller Bangor, continue an extra thirteen miles (20 kilometers) east along A2, or by bus from Carlingford to Dundalk then train to Belfast and train to Bangor. In Belfast, the tourist office (59 North St./tel. 246609) is very helpful and can book you a room. In Bangor, where I prefer the slower resort atmosphere, accommodations abound. Check the tourist office at 34 Quay St. (tel. 270069). I was comfortable at the Tara Guest House (51 Princetown Road/tel. [0247] 468924); if Tara is booked, many other inviting lodgings line this road. Spend your first day here exploring Belfast and your second day completing Walk 2 along with a tour of Bangor.

Night 4: Cushendun (Walk 3)

From Belfast head north along scenic A2 until you reach Cushendun (57 miles/92 kilometers) or take one of the not-too-frequent buses that ply the coast road. There are numerous B&Bs along the way, and you may stop at any village in the vicinity. Alternately, the tourist office at Cushendall (tel. 01266771180) can help you with local lodgings. Check into a B&B, complete Walk 3, and relax in scenic splendor during the evening.

Nights 5 and 6: Portrush or Portstewart (Walks 4 and 5)

From Cushendun continue along A6 until you reach Portrush or Portstewart (about 40 miles/64 kilometers); or via public transport you will have to return by bus to Belfast and then take a bus or train to Portrush. Lodgings abound in both towns. The tourist offices can help you, but a quick ride around town is probably just as effective. I was happily ensconced at the Calgorm B&B (117 Eglinton St./tel. 01265 823787) at Portrush. The room was comfortable but nothing special, and you will find comparable rooms at most B&Bs. Complete Walk 4 between the two towns and explore both municipalities on the first day. Head to Giant's Causeway on the second day for Walk 5 from lonely Dunseverick Castle.

Nights 7 and 8: Letterkenny (Walks 6 and 7)
Little Letterkenny stands about midway between Glenveagh Park and the Ulster-American Folk Park and is the best possible sojourn in this sparsely populated region of Ireland. As a college town it can be lively and offers many dining opportunities. The tourist office (tel. 21160) on Derry Road can help you with accommodations. From Portrush take scenic A2 through Londonderry until it becomes N13 and arrives at Letterkenny (about 60 miles / 97 kilometers). If you rely on public transport, it is best to skip Glenveagh, since there is no reliable way of reaching the park, and head south to Omagh, which is 5 miles / 8 kilometers south of the Ulster-American Folk Park, by train to Londonderry and Ulster Bus to Omagh. Drive up to Glenveagh on your first day for a superb park walk and then down to Omagh and the Ulster-American Folk Park on your second day at Letterkenny.

Night 9: Enniskillen (Walk 8)
From Letterkenny roll south along N14 to Strabane and then along A5 to Omagh where you will switch to A32 which takes you into Enniskillen (65 miles / 105 kilometers), or by bus from Omagh to Enniskillen. Enniskillen is crowded in the summer so you may wish to call ahead for reservations. Consult a comprehensive guide or call the tourist office (tel. 323110). Enjoy Enniskillen and complete Walk 8 to Station Island today.

Night 10: Ballina (Walk 9)
From Enniskillen, take N16 to Sligo and then N4 to N59 which leads you to Ballina (79 miles / 127 kilometers), or by bus to Ballina via Sligo. Enjoy the local atmosphere and take Walk 9 today.

Nights 11-13: Westport (Walks 10-12)
From Ballina drive along N57, N58, N5 and N60 to Westport (36 miles / 58 kilometers), or by bus from Ballina. Sleeping space is abundant here, and I found the Dun na Mara House on Castlebar St. (there are a variety of other lodgings available on this street) to be welcoming and comfortable (tel. 098 25205). Alternately, the tourist office, located on North Mall can be of assistance (tel. 25711). Try any of these walks in your preferred order, but if time is a factor do not miss the walk up Croagh Patrick.

If you are relying on public transportation, you may have to skip the walk at Achill Head since the buses only go up Dooagh, necessitating about a four-mile/6.4-kilometer round trip from the bus terminus to the trail head. Hitching is possible.

Nights 14 through 16: Galway (Walks 13 and 14)

Drive south from Westport along R330 until you reach Partry where you will switch to N84 and cruise directly into Galway (51 miles/82 kilometers); or take the bus from Westport to Galway. Spend the first day touring Galway; take the ferry over to Inishmore Island on the second day; and drive the 45 miles/72 kilometers over to the Cliffs of Moher on the third day (The Galway to Cork bus plys this route several times daily during the summer). Finding a room in Galway should be no problem except during special events. I stayed at the Swallow B&B at 98 Fr. Griffin Rd. (tel. 091 589073) which has several small but comfortable motel-like rooms. There are a number of other similar B&Bs along this street. There are two tourist offices where you can seek lodging assistance and purchase ferry tickets. The centrally located office is situated at Victoria Place (tel. 563081) close to Eyre Square. The Salthill office which shares the same phone number is located along the main beach.

Night 17: Limerick (Walk 15)

Tearfully departing lovely Galway, you will head east from Galway until you reach N18 and head south directly into Limerick (about 65 miles/105 kilometers); or by bus from Galway to Limerick. I sojourned comfortably at the Annesville B&B (tel. 061 452703) along Ennis Road about one mile from the city center. Other lodging opportunities can be found along this stretch, or you may consult the tourist office at Arthur's Quay (tel. 317522). Check into a B&B, take the bus out to O'Brien's Bridge, and walk back into Limerick where you may spend the evening exploring the town.

Night 18: Tralee (Walk 16)

Head west from Limerick along N69 which takes you directly into Tralee (64 miles/103 kilometers), or by bus from Limerick to Tralee. A number of B&Bs are situated along Oakpark Rd., or you can visit the tourist office at Ashe Memorial Hall on Denny St. (tel. 21288). Take the bus or taxi out to tiny Spa and enjoy an eventful walk back to lively Tralee.

Nights 19 and 20: Dingle (Walks 17 and 18)

Roll west from Tralee along N86 until you arrive at one of Ireland's most picturesque towns, Dingle (a mere 31 miles/50 kilometers), or by frequent bus from Tralee. Visit the tourist office at the intersection of Main and Dykegate (tel. 51188) for lodging assistance; or you may wish to cruise around town to select a room from numerous possibilities. Take the bus out to Lispole for a superb walk back to Dingle on the first day, and drive or take the bus out to scenic Slea Head for a second day of great walking.

Nights 21-23: Kenmare or Killarney (Walks 19-21)

From Dingle drive east along T68, changing to R561 at Anascaul until you reach N22 at Farranfore and head south until you arrive at Killarney (about 45 miles/72 kilometers); or take the bus from Dingle to Killarney. If you choose to lodge in Kenmare, continue south another 21 miles/34 kilometers along N71; or change buses at Killarney continuing to Kenmare. Both towns, especially Killarney, have numerous lodging opportunities. At Killarney, the tourist office is located in the town hall on Main St. (tel. 31067). At Kenmare you can locate the tourist office along The Square (tel. 41233). I stayed at quieter Kenmare in the Kenmare Bay Hotel, A Best Western Hotel (tel. 064 41300), and was quite satisfied. Complete Walks 19-21 in the order that best suits your choice of lodging.

Nights 24-26 Castletownbere or Kenmare (Walks 22-24)

If you have been staying at Kenmare and are content, it is possible to complete the three walks on the Beara Peninsula from your base here since the farthest destination is only about 40 miles/64 kilometers. However, if you are looking for a change in scenery or are using public transportation, Castletownbere, near the end of the peninsula is an attractive alternative. From Kenmare, head south along N71 and then west just after the bridge along R571 until you arrive at Castletownbere; or buses run from Kenmare to Castletownbere. The tourist office along the busy harbor is helpful but not always available; however, a quick ride around town will probably be sufficient to find a room—especially if you arrive early. Take the ferry over to Bere Island on the first day; visit lonely Dursey Island on the second day; and revel in one of my favorite walks anywhere, Ardgroom to Eyeries, on the third day.

Nights 27 and 28: Cork/Blarney (Walk 25)

If you are coming from Kenmare, cruise west from town along R569 until you reach N22 which goes directly to Cork (60 miles/97 kilometers). From Castletownbere, drive west along R572 until you reach N71 (at Glengarriff) which meanders to Cork (about 103 miles/166 kilometers), or by bus from Kenmare; from Castletownbere switch buses at Kenmare. I rested comfortably in Cork at the Redclyffe Guest House on Western Road (tel. 021-273220) where you will find many other B&Bs. The tourist office is located downtown along Grand Parade (tel. 273251). You may also wish to sojourn in the shadow of the great castle at Blarney or at coastal Kinsale which corners the market on picturesque tall masts around here. Explore Cork's monuments and shopping opportunities on your first day and head down to Kinsale for an evening at this lovely coastal village renowned for fine cuisine. Enjoy the nautical ambiance and a superb dining experience. On the second day, walk up to Blarney for the ritual stone-kissing ceremony.

Nights 29 and 30: Waterford (Walks 26 and 27)

From Cork roll east along N8 until you quickly intersect with N25, which eventually winds its way to Waterford (71 miles/114 kilometers), or by bus from Cork to Waterford. The Portree House on Mary St. (tel. 74574) is well appointed and accommodating. The tourist office, located at 41 Merchant's Quay, (tel. 75788) is helpful and can book throughout the area. For a more picturesque setting head down to Dunmore East, promoted justly as "Ireland's most beautiful fishing village." Try the sublimely situated Ocean Hotel (tel. 051 83576) for a fine meal and room. Visit the Waterford Crystal factory on the first day and with funds depleted head down to Tramore (frequent buses from Waterford) for a fantastic beach walk. On the second day drive up to Graiguenamanagh (public transport aficionados will have difficulty arriving here) for one of Ireland's best rambles.

Night 31: Glendalough (Walk 28)

Depart Waterford along N25 driving northeast; switch to N79 at New Ross. At Enniscorthy, take N11 to Arklow where you will begin a series of secondary roads (R747, R752, R755, and R756) that meander to Glendalough (about 82 miles/132 kilometers). You could also visit Glendalough as a day trip from Dublin but an evening amid the ethereal beauty of the Wicklow Mountains is an experience worth delaying your arrival in Dublin. If you are relying on public transportation, it is best to visit Glendalough as a day trip from Dublin (take St. Kevin's Bus Service tel. 01 281 8119). There are numerous lodging opportunities in the general area but not too many in Glendalough. Most overnighters sojourn in Laragh, a mile up the road, but there are other possibilities along R755. I very much enjoyed my stay at the simple but commodious Tochar House Bar and Lounge, which is also a B&B, in tiny Round-wood (tel. 01 281 8247).

Nights 32-40: Dublin (Walks 29-34)

From Glendalough drive along R755 until you intersect with N11, which pierces the heart of Dublin (about 30 miles / 48 kilometers). The tourist office is located at 14 Upper O'Connell St. (tel. 284 4768). There are also branch offices at Dublin Airport (same phone number) and at Dun Laoghaire along St. Michael's Wharf (same phone number). Dublin can be quite congested, and I prefer to stay away from the center of town along the Dublin rapid transit system, DART. At Howth, north of Dublin, I can recommend the well appointed Baily Court Hotel (tel. 832 2691). South of Dublin, at Dun Laoghaire, the seaside Hotel Pierre (tel. 280 0291) has comfortable but small rooms in a great location. Enjoy all of the Dublin walks and explore this intriguing capital city in depth during your last week in Ireland.

Night 41: Athlone (Walk 35)

Although I place this excursion at the end of your tour, you may wish to take a day off from Dublin at any point in your stay here. From Dublin, N4 followed by N6 will get you to Athlone (80 miles / 129 kilometers) not far from Clonmacnoise. Having booked a room in Athlone, drive back in the direction of Dublin along N6, taking a right at Fardrum along N62 until you reach Ballynahown and go right along an un-numbered road (there is a sign indicating your turn here). Frequent trains and buses depart Dublin for Athlone, and from the Athlone Castle you may take the prosaically named Mini Bus Service (tel. 0902 74839) to Clonmacnoise. This service is an all-day tour that also includes a ride on the Clonmacnoise and Offaly Railway. The tourist office safely located in the castle (tel. 94630) can help you book a room. The centrally located Prince of Wales Hotel (tel. 0902 75658) has comfortable and attractive rooms. Automobilists who do not feel like packing and unpacking can also visit Clonmacnoise as a day trip. Public transportationists can also do this as a day trip, but you must arrive early at Athlone in order to make connections with the 9:00 a.m. Mini Bus Service.

Regional Itineraries

In order to complete the regional or thematic itineraries, simply link the appropriate numbers from the Grand Tour. Some adjustments must be made in road selections; however, any general map or road atlas of Ireland will facilitate this task.

Dublin and Vicinity

Those with limited time in Ireland will probably stay in Dublin and complete the following walks, including the two great abbeys which can be done as day trips:

Walk 28: Glendalough: Grandeur in Ruin
Walk 29: Along the Royal Canal in Dublin's Hinterland
Walk 30: Dublin via the Royal Canal
Walk 31: Clondalkin to Dublin via the Grand Canal
Walk 32: Howth to Sutton via the Howth Cliff Walk
Walk 33: Dublin South: Killiney Hill Park to Dun Laoghaire
Walk 34: Dublin's Wicklow Way
Walk 35: The Great Abbey: Clonmacnoise via the Pilgrim's Road

Republic of Ireland: South of Dublin

This itinerary includes many of the most popular tourist sites and some of the finest walking anywhere in the world. This is an excellent and comprehensive itinerary for first-time travelers to Ireland.

Walk 13: Cliffs of Moher
Walk 14: Aran Islands (Galway): Inishmore Island
Walk 15: O'Brien's Bridge to Limerick
Walk 16: Spa to Tralee

Republic of Ireland: North of Dublin/Northern Ireland

Veteran travelers to Ireland who have visited many of the major tourist sites will enjoy this journey to the less visited but no less interesting northern lands. This is an excellent introduction to Northern Ireland and the unspoiled north of the Republic of Ireland.

Republic of Ireland: The West from Shannon Airport

Busy Shannon Airport (not far from Limerick) is an excellent staging point for a visit to Ireland's remote west where beauty manifests itself in wild coastal tapestries, deep forests, serpentine rivers, placid lakes, and serrated peaks. Many of Ireland's most scenic walks are located along this itinerary.

Walk 13: Cliffs of Moher
Walk 14: Aran Islands (Galway): Inishmore Island
Walk 15: O'Brien's Bridge to Limerick
Walk 16: Spa to Tralee
Walk 17: Dingle Peninsula: Slea Head to Ventry Beach
Walk 18: Lispole to Dingle
Walk 19: Killarney National Park
Walk 20: Glenbeigh: A Walk High on the Kerry Way
Walk 21: Galway's Bridge to Kenmare
Walk 22: Dursey Island
Walk 23: Bere Island
Walk 24: Beara Village Walk: Ardgroom to Eyeries
Walk 25: A Country Ramble to the Blarney Stone

Thematic Itineraries

1. Captivating Coasts and Beaches

Ireland is the home of some of the world's finest coastal scenery. The following walks highlight these remarkable natural gifts:

Walk 2: Belfast: Helen's Bay to Bangor
Walk 3: Antrim Village Walk
Walk 4: Dunseverick Castle to Giant's Causeway
Walk 5: Antrim Resort Coast: Portrush to Portstewart
Walk 10: Achill Island: A Cliff Walk
Walk 13: Cliffs of Moher
Walk 14: Aran Islands (Galway): Inishmore Island
Walk 15: O'Brien's Bridge to Limerick
Walk 17: Dingle Peninsula: Slea Head to Ventry Beach

Walk 18: Lispole to Dingle
Walk 20: Glenbeigh: A Walk High on the Kerry Way
Walk 22: Dursey Island
Walk 23: Bere Island
Walk 26: Waterford, the Crystal Palace
Walk 32: Howth to Sutton via the Howth Cliff Walk
Walk 33: Dublin South: Killiney Hill Park to Dun Laoghaire

2. Inland Waterways

The following trails follow, at least partially, the course of Ireland's beautiful lakes, rivers, and canals:

Walk 6: Glenveagh National Park
Walk 15: O'Brien's Bridge to Limerick
Walk 16: Spa to Tralee
Walk 24: Beara Village Walk: Ardgroom to Eyeries
Walk 27: Along the River Barrow
Walk 28: Glendalough: Grandeur in Ruins
Walk 29: Along the Royal Canal in Dublin's Hinterland
Walk 30: Dublin via the Royal Canal
Walk 31: Clondalkin to Dublin via the Grand Canal
Walk 35: The Great Abbey: Clonmacnoise via the Pilgrim's Road

3. Cathedrals, Churches, and Abbeys

The following walks offer the opportunity to visit Ireland's many fine religious edifices:

Walk 2: Belfast: Helen's Bay to Bangor
Walk 8: Lough Derg/Station Island
Walk 12: Croagh Patrick: A Pilgrim's Route to the Sky
Walk 15: O'Brien's Bridge to Limerick
Walk 19: Killarney National Park
Walk 21: Galway's Bridge to Kenmare
Walk 25: A Country Ramble to the Blarney Stone
Walk 28: Glendalough: Grandeur in Ruin
Walk 35: The Great Abbey: Clonmacnoise via the Pilgrim's Road

4. Obscure Villages

Irish villages are high on my list of favorite places in the entire world. Picturesque and peaceful, they will seduce you entirely—especially if pub crawling is a favored activity.

Walk 1: Carlingford: A Walk along the Tain Trail
Walk 3: Antrim Village Walk
Walk 5: Antrim Resort Coast: Portrush to Portstewart
Walk 16: Spa to Tralee
Walk 18: Lispole to Dingle
Walk 20: Glenbeigh: A Walk High on the Kerry Way
Walk 23: Bere Island
Walk 24: Beara Village Walk: Ardgroom to Eyeries
Walk 27: Along the River Barrow
Walk 28: Glendalough: Grandeur in Ruin

5. Verdant Forests

Walk 1: Carlingford: A Walk along the Tain Trail
Walk 3: Antrim Village Walk
Walk 10: Achill Island
Walk 12: Croagh Patrick: A Pilgrim's Route to the Sky
Walk 17: Dingle Peninsula: Slea Head to Ventry Beach
Walk 18: Lispole to Dingle
Walk 19: Killarney National Park
Walk 20: Glenbeigh: A Walk High on the Kerry Way
Walk 21: Galway's Bridge to Kenmare
Walk 24: Beara Village Walk: Ardgroom to Eyeries
Walk 33: Dublin South: Killiney Hill Park to Dun Laoghaire
Walk 34: Dublin's Wicklow Way

6. Isolated Islands

Although Ireland is an island, there are smaller islands off the coast where Ireland's already slow pace slackens to no pace.

Walk 18: Lough Derg/Station Island

Walk 10: Achill Island
Walk 14: Aran Islands (Galway): Inishmore Island
Walk 22: Dursey Island
Walk 23: Bere Island

7. The Must-See Itinerary: All the Great Sights

If you have a limited time in Ireland and wish to see the most famous sights while enjoying a good walk, choose from among the following:

Walk 4: Dunseverick Castle to Giant's Causeway
Walk 7: Ulster-American Folk Park/Gortin History Park
Walk 12: Croagh Patrick: A Pilgrim's Route to the Sky
Walk 13: Cliffs of Moher
Walk 14: Aran Islands (Galway): Inishmore Island
Walk 19: Killarney National Park
Walk 25: A Country Ramble to the Blarney Stone
Walk 26: Waterford, the Crystal Palace
Walk 28: Glendalough: Grandeur in Ruin
(complete any from 29-34 while in Dublin)
Walk 29: Along the Royal Canal in Dublin's Hinterland
Walk 30: Dublin via the Royal Canal
Walk 31: Clondalkin to Dublin via the Grand Canal
Walk 32: Howth to Sutton via the Howth Cliff Walk
Walk 33: Dublin South: Killiney Hill Park to Dun Laoghaire
Walk 34: Dublin's Wicklow Way
Walk 35: The Great Abbey: Clonmacnoise via the Pilgrim's Road

8. Author's Favorite Walks

The following walks were difficult to select, and they may not include the most famous sights, but in each case the walk itself is superb.

Walk 3: Antrim Village Walk
Walk 4: Dunseverick Castle to Giant's Causeway
Walk 10: Achill Island
Walk 12: Croagh Patrick: A Pilgrim's Route to the Sky
Walk 13: Cliffs of Moher

Walks-at-a-Glance

These brief summaries will help you decide which itinerary is best for you or allow you to assemble your own unique itinerary. Details for each walk can be found in Section Two.

Walk 1 **Carlingford**: *A Walk along the Tain Trail*

This is a great stop/walk between Dublin and Belfast. From the rocky-shored fishing village of Omeath, you will climb high onto Carlingford Mountain and then follow a crumbling stone fence while enjoying panoramic views through the voluminous blooming deciduous forest of the Mourne Mountains and rippling lake waters. At your terminus Carlingford, which was founded by bloodthirsty, horned-helmeted Vikings, you will enjoy inspiring relics of the Middle Ages, visiting a crumbling castle, a thought-provoking abbey, and other remnants of a bygone era. Carlingford, serenely situated on the placid shore of Carlingford Lough, is also a remote refuge from urban woes where you may quietly unwind, imbibe, and ingest.

Walk 2 **Belfast**: *Helen's Bay to Bangor*

While not entirely a media construct, Belfast's fearsome reputation is not usually deserved. Strolling about the lovely/lively Victorian city center and the University District, you will be scarcely aware of the violence that has racked this city on many occasions—no barbed wire, little or no military presence, and no bombed-out buildings. You could easily spend a couple of days here sightseeing and partaking in urban bustle. When you have bustled enough, hop on the iron horse for a quick jaunt to Helen's Bay where there is nothing to do but stare in rapt disbelief at the turgid, tormented sea and begin the trek back to Bangor. The ramble to Bangor, along a heavily used recreational band, involves trekking from beach to beach while passing an occasional World War II bunker and reveling in the extended views of green hills to your right. Lively Bangor, a many-masted, attractive port city, is a serene alternative to Belfast for a sojourn in this area. Children in particular will delight in the amusement park ambience—games, rides (try the floating swan for a unique experience), cheap souvenir shops, etc.

Walk 3   **Antrim Village Walk**: *Waterfoot (Glenariff) to Cushendun via the Ulster Way*

The Antrim coastal villages are situated at the termini of a group of nine lovely valleys known as the Glens of Antrim. Today's walk takes you through three of Antrim's finest villages: Waterfoot, Cushendall, and Cushendun. From comely Waterfoot, situated in one of the most memorable glens, you will trek high above the bay and past the disintegrating remains of Red Arch Castle as you approach winsome Cushendall where you may visit the early nineteenth-century red watch tower known as the Curfew Tower. Passing from the confines of Cushendall, you will leave civilization behind and embark upon a rustic passage amid farms, farm houses, farm animals and abandoned farm buildings—even farm fans will be farmed out. Farmland eventually cedes to forest, and the route becomes frequently alpine in appearance. Your ultimate destination, Cushendun is an indescribable haven of tranquility—a truly beautiful place blessed with lovely Georgian architecture along the banks of the North Channel and justifiably registered with the National Trust.

Walk 4 **Giant's Causeway**: *Dunseverick Castle to Giant's Causeway*

Today's walk begins at a very special place: the crumbling remains of Dunseverick Castle, which is in danger of disappearing completely, but during the Middle Ages stood as a sentinel against foreign agression. Departing Dunseverick Castle, you will almost immediately join one of the most stunning coastal paths in Ireland—towering cliffs, crashing waves, rugged shoals, and deep views into the immensity of the Atlantic Ocean are your constant companions as you trek to Northern Ireland's most popular tourist attraction, Giant's Causeway, which is billed as the eighth wonder of the world. The remarkable columns formed by a 60 million year old volcanic eruption have formed a not-to-be-missed, truly remarkable sight.

Walk 5 **Antrim Resort Coast**: *Portrush to Portstewart*

Both of today's beach towns attract hordes of tourists during July and August but are otherwise fairly quiet. Larger Portrush has a more carnival-like, youthful atmosphere, while more stately Portstewart caters to a slightly more staid clientele. Today you will stroll through Portrush's colorful town center, continue along a lovely, sandy beach, and then trek along a lonely, rock-strewn coast past one rocky, wave-beaten cove after another until you arrive at nautical Portstewart, where you may dine while gazing at a few wet-suited, die-hard surfers, struggling to remain vertical above the angry sea.

Walk 5 **Glenveagh National Park**: *A Ramble from Glenveagh Castle*

Glenveagh National Park, situated in a lovely, barely populated (except for millions of sheep) region, is reminiscent of the Scottish Highlands—lakes, mountains, and fog everywhere. Tourists come in droves to view the impressive nineteenth-century castle and its surrounding gardens.

Although the castle appears to be a relic of the Middle Ages, the interior, which has hosted such luminaries as Charlie Chaplin and Greta Garbo, exudes a commodious Victorian warmth. After touring one of Ireland's finest gardens, you will trek along the heavily forested banks of lovely Lough Beagh while clouds swirl about mysteriously and serrated peaks rise precipitously from the mist in grizzled eminence over the lake's far shore. Glance back occasionally for great views of the increasingly distant castle.

Walk 7 Ulster-American Folk Park/Gortin History Park: *Gortin to the Gortin History Park*

From tiny, one-street Gortin you will pass into one of Ireland's most verdant valleys and trace the course of a quick silver stream where bucolic serenity at its most rustic reigns supreme. Emerging from the abundantly blooming flora, you will enter the Gortin History Park where the full-scale exhibitions trace human habitation in Ireland from earliest times through the seventeenth century. Although not on today's trail, the nearby Ulster-American Folk Park is the area's primary tourist destination and one of my favorite Irish attractions. The exhibits realistically portray the story of eighteenth-century Irish emigrants' journey to America. The exhibits direct you through Ulster village, (including the home of Irish emigrant come American tycoon, Thomas Mellon), along gloomy docks, and into a ship where you will tour the densely packed living quarters to the accompaniment of genuine imitation nautical sounds and nautical motion. After a few moments, you will land in America and find yourself wandering about a pre-combustion-engine American town and eventually a Pennsylvania village.

Walk 8 Lough Derg/Station Island: *Pettigo to Station Island via the Pilgrims' Route*

From pretty Pettigo, an elfin collection of shops and homes catering mainly to pilgrims, you will stride along the main road but soon depart the world of vehicular traffic along a flowery, leafy green trail with excellent views of the surrounding hills until you attain Station Island, where the ominous sign "Saint Patrick's Purgatory" is emblazoned over the entrance to the parking lot. A visit to Station Island, one of Ireland's most important pilgrimage sites, involves three days of torture and penance during the busy months of July and August. Those accustomed to less rigorous suffering and not shamed by slacker status can go as a day tripper during the spring or fall. Even if you do not participate in a pilgrimage, Station Island is a magnificent, if not foreboding, sight that is well worth the walk.

Walk 9   A Moy Valley Excursion in County Mayo: *Killala to Ballina via the Western Way*

Killala, a lovely old seaside resort with a prominent Anglican cathedral, gains historic importance as the site of the declaration of the Republic of Ireland in 1798. Stop, have a drink, and walk away from small town Ireland on a long rural trek down the Western Way. Along this narrow band of asphalt, you will visit long abandoned Moyne Abbey which slumbers, almost forgotten along the shores of the River Moy. Back on the trail, you will marvel at the views of distant hills and soon arrive at Ireland's first Franciscan friary, Rosserk Abbey, perched majestically over the River Moy (also long abandoned and requiring a 1.5 mile/2.4 kilometer detour). As an added bonus, you will probably be there alone, since tourist buses cannot negotiate the narrow track that provides Rosserk with its only contact to the outside world. Ballina, the largest town in North Mayo and the local Bishop's seat, is attractively situated on the banks of the River Moy and caters to outdoors people, especially fishermen. Here you will find a variety of accomodations, dining opportunities, and retail options.

Walk 10   Achill Island: *A Cliff Walk*

Achill is Ireland's largest island and County Mayo's

summer playground. There are no historic monuments of note on the island so you will have time to enjoy the outside ambiance, especially the cliffs featured in today's walk. From alluring but sometimes crowded Keem Beach you will walk directly up hill away from the crowds, where grazing goats will be your only companions. Soon you will begin to trace a path along some of Ireland's most renowned cliffs while marveling at some of this ocean-bound land's most superb views. As you walk in the direction of Achill Head, the views become increasingly spectacular and the beach eventually disappears, leaving you alone in a world of crashing waves, swirling clouds, and vertiginous cliffs.

Walk 11 Westport: *Newport to Westport via the Western Way*
Leaving charming, small-town Newport (great atmosphere and an interesting church may hold you for a while) behind, you will enjoy excellent views of the town as you ascend along the river. Soon you will enter rural Ireland and course along a narrow asphalt road that often seems a tunnel of leafy trees. This bucolic trek traverses vast tracts of cultivated land and is characteristic of the tranquility that permeates County Mayo's farming communities. You will arrive in lovely Westport along a grassy path and be captivated by the attractive collection of Georgian style homes and shops pleasantly arranged along the comely banks of the Carrowbeg River and a central octagon. Outdoors people often spend time here engaged in a variety of leisure activities including horseback riding, fishing, and swimming.

Walk 12 Croagh Patrick: *A Pilgrim's Route to the Sky*
Croagh Patrick, very loftily perched above the Clew Bay, is where, according to legend, St. Patrick (after fasting for 40 days and nights) rang his bell signalling to all the snakes in Ireland that their doom was imminent. Consequently, the snakes plunged en masse to an unpleasant death, and Ireland was forever rid of the feared serpent. Today, Croagh

Patrick is a revered pilgrimage site, and thousands of pilgrims climb (some barefooted or on their knees—a remarkable, perhaps lunatic, feat of self-mortification) to the summit where there is a small church commemorating this stirring deed. The walking is tough but the views are unparalleled. Your mission, should you choose to accept it: get to the top—good luck.

Walk 13   Cliffs of Moher: *Cliff Walk*

Although remote, the Cliffs of Moher offer some of the best cliff scenery anywhere in the world. The cliffs are defined by a sheer granite wall that drops precipitously for seven hundred feet at a 180 degree angle into an invariably angry sea. Swirling eddies rise and swell at cliff's bottom as waves pound the striated cliffs. Inclement weather produces a wind-swept, almost terrifying night full of rain even at mid-day. Even a short trek along the path will result in many indelible impressions of one towering precipice after another.

Walk 14   Aran Islands (Galway): *Inishmore Island*

After disembarking at Inishmore Island, you will hop on a mini bus and speedily arrive at Dun Aonghasa, an impregnable fortress and one of Europe's finest prehistoric sites. After surveying this lofty monument, you will begin the trek across an island of barren aspect where there are not more than a few solitary trees. Ubiquitous stone fences demarcating countless green fields and thousands of fleecey sheep are your constant companions. Ocean views are unsurpassed, and in the distance, the mainland's rolling coast rises mystically in the haze even on a sunny day.

Walk 15   Limerick: *O'Brien's Bridge to Limerick*

After a quick jaunt from Limerick by bus or taxi to O'Brien's Bridge, you will survey the trail ahead and quickly descend to the canal towpath where you will experience the sights, sounds, and smells of rural Ireland and dodge the gangs of marauding sheep awaiting at strategic intervals to "baa" the unwary walker. Along the canal you will note an agglomeration of superb water lilies that Monet would have been anxious to paint. Towering gold haystacks that would have inspired Van Gogh, brush in hand, to climb over fields of French haystacks are everywhere. Approaching Limerick, you will cross the wide waters of the River Shannon and be confronted by the crumbling ruins of a castle keep and soon massive King John's Castle comes into view, marking the beginning of the transition from rural to urban. This is truly a through-the-back-door walk as you enter a major city along an almost forgotten nineteenth-century canal towpath.

Walk 16 Tralee: *Spa to Tralee*

From the semi-abandoned village of Spa you will walk quickly down to the beach and trace the sheltered coast of the Tralee Bay. This is a magnificent short walk with excellent views of the entire inlet—hills drop gently to the coast, a patchwork of earth-tone farms decorates the slopes, clouds swirl above in a sort of misty chaos, fishing vessels bounce lazily over the calm waters, and graceful swans lurk languorously at a comely freshwater pond. Along the way you can visit the completely restored and functioning Blennerville windmill and hop on the narrow-gauge, nineteenth-century Tralee Light Railway which steams (literally) the short mile and a half (2-3 kilometers) between Blennerville and Tralee. Those who choose to walk to Tralee will follow a relic of the Industrial Revolution, a canal towpath with some of the original hardware still visible. Family-oriented Tralee features one of the largest museums in Ireland, Kerry the Kingdom, where the exhibits serve as a historical narrative for County Kerry. You will also want to tour the Town Park (one of Ireland's largest) which is home to a sumptuous collection of the finest roses in the universe; and visit the Aquadome, Tralee's newest attraction, where adults may relax in a whirlpool/sauna/steamroom paradise while children bounce about a wave pool, ride rapid rapids, and tumble headlong down a giant waterslide.

Walk 17 **Dingle Peninsula**: *Slea Head to Ventry Beach*

Nature experience par excellence, this trek between wild Slea Head and mild Ventry Beach offers some of Ireland's finest scenic miles. Hollywood could find no more magnificent image for the essence of Ireland, and segments of the Tom Cruise/Nicole Kidman film *Far and Away* were filmed around Slea Head. Along the high, rocky pathway you will witness stunning views of the frighteningly ferocious Atlantic Ocean, marvel at towering hills haphazardly partitioned by jagged stone fences dropping precipitously to the coast, and contemplate prehistoric stone structures in the shape of beehives that were the humble abodes of early Christian monks. Near walk's end, you will be rewarded by expansive perspectives of lengthy Ventry Beach and quietly end a very wild Irish experience.

Walk 18 **Dingle**: *Lispole to Dingle*

Departing from veritable ghost town Lispole you will climb through a verdant passageway lined by bountifully blooming shrubbery while glancing back over your shoulder to scenes of the valley below. Trekking high beneath the shadow of mighty An Cnoc peak, you will enjoy award-winning vistas of green hills, an inviting valley, and the expansive ocean. The trail seems to have an alpine aspect about it and imparts a feeling of great loneliness even though you are never far from civilization. The final descent is along pleasant country lane with great views of Dingle Town, Dingle Bay, and distant hills. A lively, lovely place with a stream running through it, nautical Dingle sports a picturesque port where mighty masts create an artificial seagoing forest. Atmosphere is everything here, and those who savor pub life will prolong their sojourn ad infinitum in order to tour the several dozen pubs that serve less than two thousand local inhabitants.

Walk 19 Killarney National Park: *Galway's Bridge to Killarney (Muckross Abbey) via the Kerry Way*

Galway's Bridge, located at the periphery of a full blooming enchanted valley, is simply a bend in the road where you will penetrate a deeply forested narrow path and be greeted by abounding views of distant, serrated peaks. Along the way you will dodge massive, moss-covered boulders, be dazzled by overwhelming verdancy, encounter a slender, fast tumbling waterfall, trace the course of tree lined river and delight in excellent views of two lovely bodies of water, Lakes Muckross and Leane. At Muckross you will visit the magnificent nineteenth-century manor house surrounded by extensive formal gardens and stroll about the stunning remains of fifteenth-century Muckross Abbey and its surrounding cemetery. Killarney, your base, is basically a tourist town, but a very nice one—not too garish, with an astonishing number of rooms for rent at all spending levels, plenty of restaurants, some not-too-tacky souvenirs, and a great location for exploring the surrounding countryside.

Walk 20 Glenbeigh: *A Walk High on the Kerry Way*

Glenbeigh is tourist friendly but not tourist overrun, and a good day excursion for those sojourning in Killarney—the pace slackens from slow to slower. Climbing from one of Ireland's premier sandy beaches, which winds several miles around a peninsula, you will be rewarded by outstanding views of the beach and Dingle Bay. As the trail levels, you will begin a long, lonely plateau ramble that affords outstanding views of hill and dale. The views from the hilltop are realllllly BIG—you can see almost to New Jersey, and as you clamber over the final ridge, be prepared for knockout views of Glenbeigh deep in the valley below. This is a pleasant detour well off the beaten tourist track, and you will not be disappointed.

Walk 21   Kenmare: *Galway's Bridge to Kenmare via the Kerry Way*

Other tourists soon become only a memory as you scurry from Galway's Bridge to the trail where an awesome sense of preternatural calm permeates the valley and loneliness abounds. Trekking solitary across hill and dale, you will revel in privileged views available only to the walker: in the distance, gray stone and green grass vie for supremacy on mountains that recede far into the vast horizon; a fast flowing stream races alongside and great boulders litter the high country in chaotic but aesthetically pleasing disarray; curious long-abandoned structures greet you with stony silence; and near the walk's terminus you reach an apogee where vistas of Kenmare lying recumbent on its comely bay are simply astonishing. Kenmare, cozily nestled along the peaceful banks of the Kenmare River, is similar in its outdoorsy/touristy atmosphere to Killarney, but smaller and less heavily trampled. The two main streets, where facades have been attractively reconstructed, harbor a variety of savory dining opportunities and a collection of intriguing emporiums that specialize in local crafts. Combined with this not-to-be-missed walk, Kenmare offers a nonpareil overnight stop on your island tour.

Walk 22   Dursey Island: *To the End of the Beara Way*

No less beautiful and in some respects more spectacular than the Ring of Kerry is the Beara Peninsula. Here, throngs of tourists thin to a trickle, and the peninsula slumbers in tranquil obscurity. You are definitely off the beaten track, and when you reach Dursey Island, there is virtually no tourist track at all. Passage to Dursey Island is achieved via an antiquated cable car (the only one in all of Ireland) which creeps dutifully along above the crashing waves far below while providing spectacular views in all directions. Alighting briskly from the cable car, you will gratefully kiss the secure terra firma and begin to ramble along the coast. Although quite barren and almost devoid of trees, Dursey

Island has a generally green patina generously interspersed with jagged gray rocks of all descriptions. Here you will enjoy quintessential Irish panoramas on a grand scale—powerful waves crash decisively along the craggy coast; distant mainland coast and barren islands jut prominently into the horizon; low-flying birds cry out unceasingly in stentorian tones; and a few lonely fishermen ply the chronically troubled waters. Although you will traverse Kilmichael, Dursey's only hamlet, I saw no one here, making this a not-to-be-missed destination for misanthdropes—not a DROP to be found.

Walk 23 **Bere Island:** *Across the Island—from Ferry to Ferry via the Beara Way*

Castletownbere, where you will depart by ferry to Bere Island, is essentially a fishing village that has begun to attract tourists who are looking for a genuine Irish experience. Disembarkation at Bere Island signals the beginning of an intimate glimpse into the obscure, as you trek across an island seldom trodden by tourists. The already slow pace on the mainland grinds to a veritable halt here on the island. Drivers park their vehicles in the middle of the road to gossip with neighbors, secure in the realization that it could be hours before another vehicle happens along; handypeople putter endlessly in their yards; workmen stand about mutely examining the occasional pothole while contemplating the horror of future labors; normally, however, absolutely nothing at all occurs. Not only will you enjoy uncommon solitude, but a walk across the island yields uniformly excellent views of the mainland. From Bere Island's only settlement, tidy Rerrin, you will ferry back to the mainland while marveling at excellent views in all directions.

Walk 24 **Beara Village Walk:** *Ardgroom to Eyeries*

From mountain crest to serried coast, this walk is superb in all aspects—one of the best walks anywhere in Europe.

Trekking between the Beara (pronounced like Yogi's last name) Peninsula's most literally colorful towns you will be greeted by one astonishing vista after another and near psychedelic town experiences at either end. Climbing crookedly from Ardgroom, comely hills beckon your gaze, and at ridge top, neck craning in all directions, it is as if you can see the entire world in a single panoramic view. After a long trek across what appears to be a lost plateau, you will descend along the coast to iridescent Eyeries which should receive the multi-hued facade of the year award— facade colors in order of appearance (the formal arrangement of the color spectrum seems to have no import): lime green, sea green, deep blue, pale blue, light purple, bright orange, bright yellow with purple trim, beige, fuscia, deep orange, red, light yellow, light purple, pale yellow, pea green, etc., most with wildly contrasting trim. Today's trailhead, rainbow-like Ardgroom, competes fiercely (even the church is painted in a pastel purple) but lacking an adequate number of facades loses by numerical default.

Walk 25   A Country Ramble to the Blarney Stone: *Cork to Blarney*

Located on the banks of the meandering River Lee, Cork (underpopulated Ireland's second largest city with only 150,000 inhabitants) has several refined major commercial avenues encompassed by one large rough edge—industrial Ireland. If you have been crisscrossing the mall-less north country for a while, the shops of Cork, particularly along St. Patrick's Street and at the mall along Merchant's Quay, will soothe the quavering nerves of serious shoppers. As the novelty of power shopping wears thin, you may wish to visit several interesting historical sites and quaff some superb, smooth-as-silk Murphy's Irish Stout, which is brewed here, before striking out across town and into the countryside. Passing from the historic center, you will traverse a generally downtrodden area of foreboding industry, budget-oriented commerce, and hovel-like homes. This is a part of Ireland rarely seen by ordinary tourists and definitely off the beaten path. The further from the center you progress, the more suburban the setting becomes until you reach a country lane that takes you along fertile farmland, and over verdant hills while offering excellent views throughout until you reach legendary Blarney where hordes of the highly feared Dreaded Other People stand in long lines for the opportunity to osculate the Blarney Stone, an unsanitary block of limestone purported to endow the kisser with eloquent speech. I didn't stand in line for this privilege and do not feel less blessed or less eloquent. You may wish to partake in this time-honored tradition; but if not, fifteenth-century Blarney Castle and its surrounding gardens are worth the walk, as is Blarney's other main attraction, the lucrative Blarney Woolen Mills, where you can buy countless high-quality sweaters and other popular tourist fare while rubbing shoulders with the stone kissers.

Walk 26 Waterford, the Crystal Palace: *A Walk along Tramore Beach*

World-class Waterford Crystal will attract most travelers to this scenically situated port town on the River Suir. The Waterford Crystal factory, Waterford's primary attraction, draws hordes of well-heeled tourists searching for a bargain on some of the world's finest crystal. Established in 1783, it is claimed to be the largest glassworks in the world. A fast-paced, forty-five minute tour will take you from molten glass to gleaming final product. After the tour you are welcome to browse the showroom which hosts the most luminous display of crystal in the universe. From trinket-sized items to monumental masterpieces, there is something for most budgets. Elsewhere in historic Waterford there are several sights that merit a visit, but there are no walks that terminate at Waterford, so I decided to head south to the popular resort Tramore with its expansive beach and family friendly atmosphere for a sandy strand stroll. Tramore's three-mile (4.8-kilometer) beach is one of Ireland's finest and most popular. Of course, this remote, cloud-encapsuled nation is not known for its beaches, and you will not mistake Tramore for St. Tropez. You will, however, enjoy outstanding views of the ocean while listening to a stimulating symphony of crashing waves. In the distance, a friendly checkerboard pattern of forest and field encircling the entire cove greets the beachcomber/walker. Walk out as far as you wish for several memorable miles.

Walk 27   Along the River Barrow: *Borris to Graiguenamanagh via the South Leinster Way*

Cute cottages, squeaky clean shops, inviting pubs, and enticing B&B's line both sides of the Borris monostreet. Although there is not much to do here, you will want to stroll through the street on the way to the trail and perhaps be seduced through the threshold of a picturesque pub. Descending to the River Barrow's well groomed towpath, you will depart the clamor of a world increasingly dependent upon high-decible vehicular traffic and begin your time travels, luxuriating in the much slower pace of the nineteenth century when canals were a serene, silent and slow mode of transport. The canal runs along the floor of a great, green almost-primordial valley, and only the occasional farmhouse hanging from the slopes in the distance is reminiscent of encroaching civilization. To your right, the canal's waters ebb indolently but tenaciously while on the left the luxuriant blanket of sparkling wild flowers and dense shrubbery creeps to water's edge; overhead drift the ubiquitous songs of shiny, happy birds who intermingle with amiable butterflies flitting about to and fro. This is a uniformly enchanting ramble into one of Ireland's most enticing villages, Graiguenamanagh. This tiny patch of isolated urbanity began its existence during the thirteenth century as Duiske Abbey. Today, farm vehicles lumber regularly along the town's narrow streets which provide all the amenities of rural Ireland—pubs, shops, lodgings— all housed in the architecturally interesting stone structures that line the narrow streets. It is also a great place to raise children who fish, climb hills, and explore paths with carefree nonchalance. Although not far from bustling Waterford, you are far from the madding crowd.

Walk 28 Glendalough: *Grandeur in Ruin*

Today's superb trek to one of Ireland's most impressive historical attractions begins at tiny Annamoe where you will begin a gentle climb through the ancient, stone-fenced farmland that almost envelopes the town. In the distance, your eyes will be drawn to the lovely pine-covered Wicklow Mountains, which extend ad infinitum into the horizon. The land here is rolling, alluring, extremely pacific, and beyond the ubiquitous, enthusiatically grazing sheep who shed wool everywhere, you will have this enchanted landscape to yourself. The final river walk (one of my favorite stretches anywhere) to Glendalough is archetypically Irish green. Everything—stone fences, trees, rocks, etc.—endures an all-encompassing moss. Approaching Glendalough, you will be greeted by sublime views of the ruins available only to the walker and then cross quickly over a swift river to Ireland's premier monastic site. First inhabited by the hermit St. Kevin during the sixth century, Glendalough soon grew into a massive complex inhabited by hundreds of monks. Although extensive, what remains is only a fraction of the original site. Visit the towering 100-foot, twelfth-century Round Tower and the impressive cathedral, which is the largest monastic structure still partially intact and once the largest cathedral in Ireland. Many other historic structures still stand against the ravages of time, and there is a most picturesque cemetery providing an exceptionally pleasant abode for the dead and a pause for reflection on so many lost memories of the past; many of the stones (Celtic crosses here, there, and everywhere—and tilting at all angles) are now mute, their messages slowly erased by the inexorable passage of time. There is no finer destination for a great day of walking through time.

Walk 29 **Along the Royal Canal in Dublin's Hinterland**:
Leixlip to Maynooth via the Royal Canal
Today you will be only about fifteen miles (24 kilometers)
from Dublin but a world apart. Although no one ever stops
here, Leixlip, attractively set along the River Liffey with a
thriving commercial sector, is a very busy little town in its
own right with increasing numbers of citizens who commute to Dublin via numerous daily trains and buses. There
is not much to do here so the urban weary will want to
head straight to the canal for a lonely but lovely walk. The
towpath trek provides a very attractive park-like atmosphere—waterlillies and wild flowers bloom; dense foliage encroaches; fishermen escaping family responsibilities
while away hours ad infinitum; and, as a bonus, you will
probably see and hear a couple of trains rumble by intent
on some far off destination. Near walk's end Maynooth's
church spire appears over the canal; and, like most towns,
Maynooth appears so much grander when you approach
it with great satisfaction on foot. Maynooth Castle, constructed during the twelfth century, is the town's most
popular tourist attraction. It stands picturesquely in ruins
along the main street awaiting your visitation. St. Patrick's
College (the oldest Catholic seminary in Ireland), adjacent
to the castle, is also worth a visit. The visitor's center conducts tours of the venerable structures, which are surrounded by alluring gardens. After your mini-tour, eat,
drink, and hurtle back to Dublin on the train for a night of
riotous pleasure in the big city.

Walk 30 **Dublin via the Royal Canal**: *Castleknock Station*
to Downtown Dublin
The Royal Canal, constructed during the late eighteenth
century, links Dublin with the River Shannon about ninety
miles away. Today you will traverse the canal towpath's
final few miles into Dublin and experience Ireland's capital city as a Dubliner rather than a tourist. Starting from
the far reaches of exurbia, you will ramble through the

good, bad, and ugly that great cities conceal from all but the most cognizant travelers. Trekking from Castleknock Station and beneath superhighway M50, you will begin what is essentially a rural trek through a major metropolis. Nowhere in the middle of somewhere is an apt description—road sounds in the distance are often your only link to modernity. Along the way, you will stride beneath still-functioning, eighteenth-century bridges; be dazzled by frequent stands of wild flowers along the often heavily treed banks; spy rabbits that appear briefly before scurrying back into the bushes (not desirous of becoming dinner for some insensitive rambler); savor the suavely sophisticated swans that float regally along the canal; and peer into the waters which are becoming choked by plant life (although still navigable) and needs to be dredged. Continuing along, suburban and rural begin to interwine as subdivisions abruptly appear as if recently willed by some higher being; foreboding factories and warehouses, uninvitingly encased in voluminous reels of razor wire, rise regularly from the boundaries of the canal, indicating the increasingly urban nature of the walk; and graffiti is scrawled on any available concrete—"FREE ALL POLITICAL PRISONERS," "MICKEY, CHARLIE, ETC." were here, "MORO LOVES SUZ" and the like ad nauseum. No other guidebook will take you on a walk like this, into the heart of the real Dublin through the real back door.

Walk 31 Dublin via the Grand Canal: *Clondalkin to Downtown Dublin*

This is a very eventful six miles (10 kilometers) right into the heart of Dublin from the middle of absolutely nowhere. You will descend from the train at Clondalkin, a nondescript industrial/commercial area that is nowhere near the beaten tourist track and stride immediately to the nineteenth-century Grand Canal. Dublin is often revealed at its least attractive along this somewhat disturbing trek that stands in pointed contradiction to the usual bucolic serenity encountered in Ireland. With cyclopean electrical towers looming overhead, you will pass an attractively appointed junkyard; survey makeshift dumps here and there; and puzzle over unsightly warehouses girdled by aesthetically arranged coiled steel and barbed wire as protection from urban marauders. Eventually departing the canal, you will begin to traverse the people's Dublin and course along streets that harbor rows of townhouses and apartment buildings punctuated by diminutive shops and local restaurants. You will also pass the Guinness Brewery on James Street where you may stop for a tour, souvenirs, and a refreshing drink straight from the sacred source. Approaching Trinity College, you will be in the heart of historic Dublin, and shoulder to shoulder with less adventurous tourists, but you can be certain that no one else has been where you have been. You have experienced a fascinating six-mile transition which illustrates that in European cities (in distinct contrast to American cities) wealth is still concentrated at the city center while the impecunious are relegated to the fringes or hidden beyond the pale.

Walk 32   Dublin/Howth Peninsula: *Howth to Sutton via the Howth Cliff Walk*

Howth lies at the end of a peninsula about ten miles (16 kilometers) north of downtown Dublin along the Dublin Bay via Dublin's rapid transit system, DART. This is a superlative destination for flight from Dublin's harried pace. Here you can relax at a waterfront restaurant while enjoying the catch of the day that has been trawled from the sea only hours ago, wander along the calm, village-like streets, and visit several interesting attractions that may delay your cliff walk. The trek out of town takes you past an armada of fishing boats intermingled with pleasure craft where you will soon merge with the trail along a rocky, boulder-stewn beach. Along the ever winding trail, the sea is virtually ubiquitous with views only occasionally obscured by dense foliage. Plying the choppy waters are frequent freighters, elegant sail boats, and an occasional three-masted schooner. Farther along, one craggy promontory after another marks the trail while brilliantly effusive wild flowers cling tenuously to the steep cliffs. Crumbling, foliage-covered walls appear regularly, and there are a number of opportunities to descend from the trail to sandy beaches which are generally very secluded. You will also pass powerfully situated Baily Lighthouse, inspect a nineteenth-century martello tower and arrive at commodious Sutton just in time for a much needed pint of Guinness.

Walk 33 Dublin South: *Killiney Hill Park to Dun Laoghaire via the Dun Laoghaire Way*

Killiney Hill Park, just south of Dublin and covering most of tall Dalkey Hill, requires a precipitous climb as soon as you descend from the bus. However, ascending to the hilltop obelisk (constructed during the mid-eighteenth century), you will be astonished by distant views of seemingly endless beaches to the south and long vistas of the sea merging mistily with remote Wales along the horizon. Along the way, you will pace through hyper-green Killiney Hill Forest, revel in glimpses of luxurious lodgings that were built for the Dublin elite early in this century, visit elegant Dalkey Village (Bernard Shaw's childhood home), inspect twelfth-century Bulloch Castle, stride sandy beaches into the expansive docks that serve as the principal port for traffic from Great Britain, visit the National Maritime Museum, and stop at the Sandycove martello tower (where Joyce stayed briefly in 1904) that houses the James Joyce Museum. This is a uniformly satisfying walk that you will not want to miss.

Walk 34 Dublin's Wicklow Way: *Marlay Park to Glencullen via the Wicklow Way*

Beloved by Dubliners, Marlay Park is a captivatingly beautiful park with vast open spaces, dense forests, open air art, innumerable benches and an air of preternatural calm—

a great place to lounge leisurely on a solar friendly afternoon. You will soon leave the locals behind and traverse the heavily forested park path until you leave the park along Kilmashogue Lane while enjoying the startlingly distant views of Dublin (the greatest panoramas of a capital city that I have ever been privileged to view), Dublin Bay, the Howth Peninsula and beyond. Continuing upward, you will cut through a very fragrant coniferous forest before emerging to an entirely different but equally spectacular set of views—Dublin disappears but is replaced by astonishing views of the seemingly endless Wicklow Mountains. The hilltop descent continues to astonish until valley floor is attained and you arrive at Glencullen, which is basically two golf courses and the popular Johnny Fox's Tavern.

Walk 35 The Great Abbey: *Clonmacnoise via the Pilgrim's Road*

Clonmacnoise, situated along a lovely bend of the River Shannon, rivals Glendalough in beauty of site and structures. Founded during the mid-sixth century by St. Kieran, Clonmacnoise grew steadily into a massive complex of religious structures and monks' quarters. The present-day religious complex with its numerous Celtic crosses and venerable religious structures (the oldest structures date from the ninth century) scattered aesthetically along the verdant banks of the River Shannon, is a magnificent sight which you will want to savor slowly. Forcing yourself to pass from these mystical grounds, you will begin a trek along the Pilgrim's Road, which was named for the great waves of the faithful who swept along its hallowed path during important holy days. Along the way, you will visit the diminutive, twelfth-century Nun's church, enjoy excellent views of the river swirling gracefully along its tangential course, traverse a tranquil, rolling, green landscape, and marvel at inspiring views of Clonmacnoise as you begin the return walk.

Part One
Hitting the Trail

1. Before You Leave

Other Travel Guides

The stolidly written but very useful green Michelin Guides provide a good general overview of Ireland. Each has a map in the front that rates the importance of all the sites, major and minor, within a certain region. They also have sections relating to history, culture and specific monuments. I am often surprised to find even the most obscure places mentioned and do not hesitate to consult these guides when I am formulating walking and driving routes. They can be purchased in bookstores everywhere and are moderately priced.

When a traveling companion purchased a *Let's Go: Europe* many years ago, I humored her by saying that it was a good idea. What I actually thought was that it was a waste of money, and I had nothing to learn from a cabal of callow college students. Before going to Europe that summer I deigned to regard only the book's covers, shunning the contents. Slowly, while driving, as my companion continued to stridently bark out many useful bits of information I was converted. At first I would steal glances at a page or two; later I found myself reading whole chapters. Now I would consider no trip without a copy. When I read one of these volumes, I want to leap from my couch, strap on a backpack, throw away (or perhaps just hide) my credit cards, and travel cheaply to all of these wonderful and charming places. Of course the feeling soon passes. I regain my senses, and I check my wallet for the reassuring sight of a credit card. I highly recommend purchasing *Let's Go: Ireland* (New York: St. Martin's Press, annual). I have seen no other guide that contains so much information on train/bus schedules, tourist offices, places to change money, laundromats, restaurants, and much more.

I would also recommend the various guides published by Arthur Frommer, especially if you are looking for more upscale dining and accommodations. However, as I will soon discuss, finding lodging in

Ireland is usually not a problem.

For a fascinating overview of the history of Ireland as it relates to the modern traveler, I strongly recommend Interlink Publishing's *A Traveller's History of Ireland*. This compact volume offers a complete and authoritative history from the earliest of times up to the present day. A gazetteer cross-referenced to the main text pinpoints the historical importance of many of the sights and towns you will encounter on your walks.

Until I read Colin Fletcher's *Complete Walker*, my few desultory attempts at backpacking and wilderness walking were singularly unsuccessful. This book changed my walking life and made me a successful outdoorsperson. I hope future editions come bundled with bionic knees which would also help. Even if you are only contemplating a walk through a city park, you will probably find some useful tips. Every conceivable topic is exhaustively treated. I recommend this book for backpackers and day hikers. Wonderfully written in idiosyncratic "old codger" prose, the *Complete Walker III* (New York: Alfred A. Knopf, 1986) should be found in every walker's bookcase.

Level of Fitness

If you are already a regular walker, you should have no problem with any of the walks listed in this book. None of the walks require any serious climbing, but a few involve a number of breathtaking ups and downs. In the trail notes, I have listed the approximate amount of climbing that you will do on each trail. If you are not a frequent walker and not involved in an exercise program, you should begin walking regularly a couple months before you arrive in Ireland. The walks that I have included vary from about two to nine miles (3 to 14 kilometers), with most ranging from three to six miles (5 to 10 kilometers). If you can walk four to five miles (6.4 to 8 kilometers) before you leave, you should be able complete all of the walks I have listed. There are a number of books that show you how to develop a walking-fitness program. I have never been able to read more than a few pages of such books and find it odd that so much ink has been devoted to such a simple and natural motion. I just begin with a few three-to-five-mile (5 to 8 kilometer) walks and increase the distance until I reach the maximum length of walk that I anticipate completing. At this level of walking fitness, I adjust quickly to walking in Ireland.

Car Rental

If you have decided to drive, you should reserve a car before you leave for Ireland. Renting a car once you have arrived in Ireland is substantially more expensive. I always find the cheapest and most fuel-efficient vehicle. For up to three people who are not large and do not bring much luggage, the smallest vehicles are sufficient. It is best to comparison shop for rates, but my lengthy and tight-fisted study gave the economy award to Alamo (1-800-327-9633) whose rates and service were more than satisfactory. To avoid paying expensive collision insurance, use a gold or platinum type credit card that covers your rental vehicle in the case of accident or theft. Call your credit card company for details which can vary.

When to Go

Most people will go during the summer, but Ireland's moderate climate allows for walking throughout most of the year, although you may not enjoy a northern coastal walk in March when the wind is howling and the mist is rising.

What to Bring

Money

With the less-than-impressive dollar hovering around 1.6 Irish Pounds, I budget about $80 to $90 dollars per day if I am traveling alone, including lodging, meals, snacks, gasoline, and admissions fees (usually staying in bed and breakfasts with private bath facilities and eating moderately-priced meals). I find that an extra person adds about $40 to $50 dollars to the expenses adding up to about $120 to $140 per day. It is possible to travel for much less by using public transportation and finding the least expensive bed and breakfasts or hostels (for information on how to travel more cheaply, consult the *Let's Go* budget guide mentioned above). I usually carry about $400 dollars worth of Irish Pounds in cash for minor purchases or emergencies, and the rest of which I plan to spend in American Express travelers checks for cash replenishment or for payment of lodgings and meals. I also charge some meals and hotels, but Visa, Mastercard, and American Express cards are not always accepted especially at lodgings and restaurants in the budget category. However, even if you are a high-budget traveler, you should always have some cash available in more remote areas and in case computer lines are down and your credit card is not approved.

Luggage

I bring one backpack which serves as check-in luggage. It carries almost everything except books, guides, maps and other expensive or indispensable items. You may wish to purchase a pack that has a disappearing suspension system as an alternative to a wilderness pack. Ordinary luggage with only a handle looks pathetically useless to me and, unless you have porters or are on a guided tour, they should be shunned.

I use what will be my hiking daypack as carry-on luggage. I own a Lowe Klettersack which is incredibly durable, comfortable and capacious. I will discuss the use and selection of a daypack in a following section. My third piece is a small shoulder bag that contains photographic equipment, mini cassette recorder and a few other small items. When I arrive at the airport or park my car, I put the large pack on my back, strap the camera bag around my neck, hold the daypack with both arms, and stagger to my destination. I avoid bringing more than I can carry in one trip.

Clothing

Not including what I am wearing on the plane, I bring four shirts, two pairs of pants, one pair of shorts, three pairs of regular socks, three pairs of wool hiking socks, four pairs of underpants, one hat, one sweater, one lightweight jacket, one pair of hiking boots, one pair of walking shoes and one pair of sandals. Everything is color coordinated and can be easily washed and dried. Although I become quickly tired of these clothes, they are sufficient for months of touring and can be easily burned upon return from Ireland.

Personal/Health Items

Always bring soap if you are a budget traveler since some low cost lodgings do not feel obligated to assure that their clients are sparkling clean. I also bring multiple vitamins which I usually forget to take, razors, scissors, dental floss, thick dental tape which I use to remove trapped, broken dental floss from between my teeth, toothbrush/paste, Ace Bandages for possible sprains, aspirin or aspirin substitute, bandaids and toilet paper which you should keep in your day pack in case of emergency. I do not bother with shampoo or conditioner, but you may have more hair and find bar-soap to be an inadequate hair cleanser.

Miscellaneous

Sewing needles and thick thread are useful for torn clothes, lost buttons, and damaged equipment. I always bring a high-quality small flashlight that runs on AA batteries to fend off uninvited darkness. An extra, easily-compressed small backpack is convenient for shopping around town and carrying laundry. I also carry a small towel that I have not yet employed for any task; however, I fear excluding it from my pack because I suspect that it will, at an unspecified future date, rescue me from some acute emergency situation. A small am/fm radio may break the silence of a televisionless budget B&B room. A light-weight electronic alarm will prod you from bed and ensure promptness to important transportation occurrences. I never go on any trip, foreign or domestic, without a lightweight goosedown sleeping bag. I have a North Face Light Rider, which weighs about two pounds and compresses to almost invisibility. A sleeping bag makes an excellent extra blanket and is indispensable when unrolled in its large storage sack as an extra large pillow which can allow you to sit comfortably upright on a bed with your head against the wall or headboard.

Daypack

On day hikes, I carry a Lowe Klettersac which, as I have mentioned, is strong and durable. It has a top pocket and is also large enough to carry the numerous items I am about to mention. The Klettersac also has a narrow waistbelt, which distributes some of the weight from my shoulders to my hips. The waistbelt also prevents the pack from shifting at some critical juncture where I might be sent hurtling into an uninviting abyss. Even if you are not carrying much weight, be certain to purchase a pack with well-padded straps and a waistbelt.

I am not able to enjoy a simple walk without a vast catalog of items that are designed to ward off any and every conceivable problem. I envy the occasional person I see strolling down a remote trail wearing a disintegrating pair of sandals and carrying nothing more than a leaking bottle of mineral water. I have never had the spiritual levity that allows these people to face possible disaster or even discomfort with such nonchalance.

The items you select from the following list for your daypack will depend upon where you fall on the nonchalance/paranoia continuum. I will discuss my rationale for carrying and frequency of use for each item.

The most important item in or on your daypack is water. I prefer the taste of water that is carried in clear, unbreakable lexan bottles with a loop top that prevents the tragedy of lost bottle caps. I use the one-liter size that can be inserted into nylon bottle-holders. The bottle-holders have a velcro loop that can be placed over belts, and I loop one around an adjustment strap on the side of my pack. Depending on the length of the walk, I also carry one or two extra bottles in the pack where they stay cooler. Do not pick up a bottle of mineral water, throw it in your pack, and assume that you have a safe supply of water; they are very flimsy and any dropped pack will mean bottle breakage. Use only indestructible water containers, and do not lose them.

Powdered water additives such as Gatorade can be purchased in many larger supermarkets. They strike me as being expensive, but on longer, electrolyte-unbalancing walks I occasionally use them. They are also useful if you become weary of the taste of plain, warm water.

On most walks, you will carry food. I usually bring some type of whole-grain bread, and I always have a supply of emergency *gauffrettes*. *Gauffrettes* are the chocolate or vanilla wafers that cause me to gain several pounds during a summer of walking. Most people have more sophisticated culinary desires and will be pleased with the variety of foods available even in smaller stores. For me, picnics involve too much organizing and general psychological stress. However, I realize that not everyone is going to find happiness sitting on a rock while gnawing on a loaf of bread.

I suspect that the concept of ozone depletion is actually a massive conspiracy by the world's sunscreen manufacturers; but, like an atheist who prays occasionally at bedtime, I am not sure and prepare for all possible outcomes. I do not like the slippery feel of sunscreen, and I still cannot bring myself to smear it on my balding, some say bald, head. However, I usually remember to put it on my face and arms. The best I have found is Coppertone's Sport SPF 30, which clings tenaciously to my skin rather than dripping into my eyes. However, if the price escalates from the present $7 for four ounces, only the wealthiest of walkers will be able to afford its protection. Purchase sunscreen before you leave; in Ireland it is even more expensive.

Although I seldom have blisters, I always include a package of Dr. Scholl's Moleskin in my daypack. Moleskin and similar products marketed by Spenco, attach to the skin in order to prevent sensitive spots from becoming blisters through frequent rubbing against a boot. I have used Moleskin on several occasions, and it has saved me from some painful miles. I also carry a small pair of scissors to properly shape the Moleskin.

As I mentioned before, toilet paper should always be kept within arm's reach. There are few toilets on trails and even fewer with toilet paper. Since toilets and reading material are frequently associated items, I should mention that I always bring a book, magazine, or newspaper on a walk. You may be trapped in a situation where you must wait for public transportation (The combination of nothing to do and nothing to read, sends me into an uncontrolled panic), or you may find an alluring spot that begs you to peruse that *Time* magazine whose covers you have been dying to get between.

I have lightweight binoculars that usually stay in my pack. Although they are seldom used, they can be valuable on less-frequently-marked trails that cross many treeless, rockless open fields. Binoculars enable you to scan distant rocks and trees for waymarks.

A mini-cassette recorder can be useful for recording thoughts and experiences while on the trail. I also use it to record trail sounds such as singing birds, quick moving rivers, and occasional conversations.

It frequently rains in Ireland, so you will need to pack a poncho or other rain protection. Do not leave it behind on sunny days; weather can change quickly in Ireland—a fact that I have learned the hard way after having been deeply saturated on a long poncholess walk. Even in summer, the weather can be cool and you will probably wish to bring a lightweight jacket.

A map pouch that you can suspend from your body is also indispensable. Silva and other companies make a variety of these pouches, which should be waterproof and fasten with velcro tabs. They keep your maps and guides visible but dry and also store a variety of other small items.

Trail Garb: Not GQ

I usually wear lightweight cotton pants and shirts, but during the summer, I often wear shorts. Although almost all of the trails in this book are in good condition, your uncovered legs may suffer abrasive attacks on some segments.

Since jogging or walking shoes do not offer tender soles enough protection from the frequently rocky trails, hiking boots usually adorn my valuable feet. I own two pairs of Vasque Sundowners which currently retail for about $180. They are leather with a waterproof Gore-Tex lining and do not weigh heavily on my feet. They are the most comfortable boots that I have owned, but the soles seem to last only one summer. They can be resoled for about $50. If you do not currently own hiking boots, I suggest that you try several pairs before making a final decision.

Although I usually wear boots on the trail, I am always in a hurry to remove them when I have completed a walk. If I have a car waiting for me at the end of the trail, I leave a pair of walking shoes or sandals in the trunk and change as soon as possible. If I am taking public transportation back to my hotel, I endure the hiking boots until I return since they are too bulky to comfortably fit into my daypack.

I have both cotton and wool hiking socks. Both are comfortable, but I almost always wear the wool socks. I have no scientific explanation for this choice. I also have a hat which, unless it is raining, is found in my pack. A poncho and lightweight jacket, which I have already mentioned, complete my walking wardrobe.

2. When You Get There

Where to Stay

It is usually possible to find a room through the local tourist offices or occasionally via reservations services at airports and train stations. If you feel insecure without prior reservations, check the listings in the guides I have recommended. I do not like to be too precise about when I am going to be somewhere, so I generally just look around town when I arrive or head straight to the tourist office. Never, even in the height of the summer season in popular areas, have I gone shelterless. Usually the first place I check has an available room. However, if you are on a strict budget or are using public transportation to travel around Ireland, you may wish to make reservations. I have included some specific recommendations in the Grand Tour Itinerary section that I believe are quite worthy of mention.

Food and Drink

Your culinary experience in Ireland is not likely to be a series of haute cuisine adventures, but the food is good and substantial. Variety is not the spice of life here, especially for breakfast eaters. The almost invariable Irish breakfast, served in most B&Bs and hotels, consists of fried everything—eggs, potatoes, sausage, bacon, etc. You will often start with cereal, juice, and milk. Those who wish to avoid soaring cholesterol levels will also end at this first course. I frequently skip this traditional morning (soon to be mourning) ritual in favor of delicious freshly baked scones purchased at a local bakery. I often eat scones for lunch also, but no self respecting Irish person would share this idiosyncratic infatuation for baked goods throughout the day's duration. Lunch and dinner are usually taken in pubs or restaurants (although most Irish eat at home unless they are touring) where the food is generally plentiful and appetizing. Most meals are served with potatoes; if you consider potato famine to be a blessing, you will probably lose weight in Ireland. I enjoy fresh fish on a regular basis, but search (usually in vain) for vegetarian fare; however, pubs and restaurants that serve standard Irish fare are starting to boldly explore meatless and ethnic cuisine with decidedly mixed results. Ethnic restaurants are also beginning to take root here and there. I have eaten in Chinese, Indian, and Mexican restaurants that were quite good, but these are found only in larger population centers or areas that cater mainly to tourists.

Regardless of what is eaten, it is usually accompanied by Guinness Stout—Ireland's national drink and source of pride on an international scale. In fact, I have had several Irish explain with non-feigned straight faces that export Guinness (even in the draught version) is inferior to what the Irish keep for themselves—"We have the best Guinness" is a quote that you will likely hear. You cannot leave this island without a pint or hundreds of pints of this great brew. Other great beers are also available. I like Murphy's Irish Stout which is brewed in Cork. Murphy's has a smoother body but a rather elusive taste which I seem to enjoy more with food, while I tend to enjoy Guinness more when drinking for the sake of drinking. Less potent brews are also available, and if you prefer lagers, the most popular is the Harp, which is brewed by Guinness. Bland, uninteresting American beers are also becoming available, mainly in Dublin. Do not waste calories on these worthless non-entities when real beer is available around virtually every corner.

Public Transportation

Almost all of these linear walks have been designed so that you will have the opportunity to be involved in short trips on public transportation, which introduces you into the life of small-town Ireland. On rural buses, in particular, you will often believe that you have entered the driver's living room as he is entertaining guests. The regulars converse among themselves and the driver passing along the latest gossip. Buses, unlike trains however, are not always on time. Although they almost always appear, you should wait at least 30-40 minutes before abandoning hope. Complete instructions for necessary local transportation are included in the trail notes for each walk.

Driving

Even though escape from cars and traffic is one of the goals of a walking vacation, there is no inconsistency in writing about driving in a walking book. Ironically, your car will enable you to more efficiently avoid other cars and also give you the freedom to set your own schedule. You will be free from crowded long-distance public transportation and able to reach places that are not served by public transportation. Although there are some negatives including expense, occasional heavy traffic, difficult parking in large cities, and some poorly marked roads, I would not enjoy Ireland as much without the freedom a car allows.

Roads in Ireland are usually two lanes which means that you will average, at best, 35 to 40 miles (56 to 64 kilometers) per hour. You cannot be in a hurry except approaching or departing Dublin where there are several divided highways for rapid ingress and egress to and from this capital city. There are a few miles/kilometers of divided highway around other major population centers, but it will be decades before the nation is connected by a comprehensive network of high-speed dual carriageways. However, even if there were fast roads throughout Ireland, I would recommend travel on backroads. In fact, when there are faster alternatives, the backroads will be even more desirable since trucks and other undesirables will be few and far between. Car crawling along the narrow asphalt and concrete bands that link the towns and villages is part of a complete Irish experience, almost on a par with pub crawling. Automobile travel through this serene island is an astonishing tableau of everchanging scenic sublimity with ever winding roads guiding you through fertile fields, rolling hills, jagged peaks, and along superb stretches of some of the finest coastal scenery anywhere.

Communication

If you are going to use telephones in Ireland, purchase a telephone card which, unless you are calling an emergency number or the operator, you must insert into most pay phones in order to complete a call (coin-operated phones are still encountered, particularly in rural areas, but will soon go the way of carrier pigeons). Cards can be purchased at newsagents, post offices, and Eason bookshops/stationery stores. Follow the directions on the phone, which will consist of inserting your card and dialing. For long distance calls to the United States, you may access an American operator from AT&T (1-800-550-000 in the Republic of Ireland; or 0800-890-011 in Northern Ireland) or MCI (1-800-551-0001; or 0800-890-222 in Northern Ireland). Calls cost about $1.25 per minute, so borrow a friend's code number or be prepared to sell personal property when you return from Ireland.

Letters take between one to two weeks to reach the USA from Ireland. If you wish to mail a letter or post card from Ireland, go the local post office where you may purchase stamps and usually envelopes.

3. Trail Life

Waymarking

Waymarking is the practice of placing indicators (usually a variety of colored paints) on natural objects such as trees or stones to aid hikers in finding their way. Sign posts with arrows and other indicators are also used on some trails.

The trails in this book represent some of the finest walking available anywhere in Europe, and I have made every effort to find the best trails that are either near great tourist attractions, are attractions themselves—meaning people come to the region to hike, or they take you to interesting off-the-beaten-track areas. The selected trails are either waymarked or easy to follow without being marked. Follow the directions in the trail notes, and you will not get lost. Finally, do not be afraid to get off the beaten path; I have been lost all over Europe and negative events have never occurred. In fact, as you are able to surmise, I have always found my way back. With the aid of this book, you too will always find your way back after many a backcountry adventure.

Use of Trail Notes and Optional Maps

All of the walks can be completed without the purchase of additional maps; however, wherever possible, I have recommended maps that will be of use to you, particularly if you are planning to go beyond the walks recommended in this book. All of these maps are topographical meaning they use what are called "contour lines" to give a detailed picture of how the land is shaped. If you know how to read a topographical map, you will be able to visualize where, how often, and how steeply you must climb on each walk. You will also be able to locate natural features such as lakes and rivers and man-made objects such as buildings and utility wires.

You should also purchase a compass with a transparent, rectangular base plate that can be used in conjunction with a topographical map. They are inexpensive and can always indicate in what direction you are traveling. If you follow the trail notes in this book, you will not need a compass. However, if you experiment with other trails or absent-mindedly wander off the trails described in this book, there is always the possibility of becoming lost. Knowing how to use a map and compass has helped me stay found on a number of occasions.

If you purchase a Silva or Suunto brand compass, brief instructions for its use will be included. Study these instructions, and attach them with a rubber band to the compass so that they will be with the compass when you need to review them. There are a number of books that offer instruction in the use of map and compass. *Staying Found* by June Fleming (New York: Vintage, 1982) is clearly written and will teach you more than you ever wished to know about staying found. Many other comparable books can be found in the hiking section of your favorite bookstore.

If you do not learn from books, try orienteering. This is a rapidly growing international competitive sport. You are given a map and are required to find your way as quickly as possible through varied terrain. Along the way you must record certain codes that will prove that you have touched all points on a required route. There are several levels of competition, and novices are welcome. For more information, contact the United States Orienteering Federation, P.O. Box 1444, Forest Park, GA 30051.

If you are anxious to order any of the optional Ordnance Survey maps recommended in the final section prior to arrival in the Republic of Ireland, contact the Ordnance Survey Office, Phoenix Park, Dublin 8, Ireland (tel: 01-8206100; fax: 01-8204156). For Northern Ireland contact the Ordnance Survey of Northern Ireland, Colby House, Stranmillis Court, Belfast BT9 5BJ, Northern Ireland. The tourist bureaus also have general information about walking. Request a packet of information including walking opportunities using the following toll-free numbers: Irish Tourist Board (Bord Failte) 1-800-223-6470 and the Northern Ireland Tourist Board 1-800-326-0036. If you wish to purchase maps after your arrival in Ireland, it is a good idea to shop at the Ordnance Survey offices mentioned above or at one of the larger bookstores in Dublin. Maps and guides are not always available in smaller towns.

How Often/How Far

I have included walks that are anywhere from two-to-nine miles (3.2 to 14.4 kilometers) with most in the three-to-six-mile range (4.8 to 9.6 kilometers). Even if you only embark on an occasional short walk, you will experience Ireland as have few other visitors.

Do not become obsessed with distance. This is not a competitive sport, and there is no point in consuming entire days with walking. You are on vacation and should enjoy not only the walks but the destinations. A three-to-six-mile walk (4.8 to 9.6 kilometers) will take you into the countryside and onto local public transportation for several hours. You will also have gotten enough exercise to justify a calorie-laden dinner and will be tired enough to sleep well at night. Also remember that you will often be walking several miles around tourist sites and your home base during the evening. A day in which you complete a six mile (9.6-kilometer) walk can easily add up to a ten-mile (16-kilometer) walking day with such incidental walking.

Time of Day

In less traveled areas, you will occasionally have to arrange your walking schedule around available transportation. However, many areas have excellent public transportation and you can often arrange the walks to fit your general schedule.

When I have a choice, I usually stagger onto the trail at about ten or eleven a.m. This is in contrast to conventional wisdom which counsels early rising in order to beat the midday heat. Since I am never in any hurry to rise early and rush to any destination, I spend many days walking in the noon-day sun with only the occasional mad dog or Irishman as a companion.

Problems

Ireland's trails are almost always havens of tranquility with nothing to fear but fear itself. Your right to walk unmolested through the countryside is universally respected. You may trek without trepidation.

The Car: Where to Leave It

I prefer to leave the car at my final destination and take the bus or train back to my walk's starting point. This procedure assures me that my car, barring theft, will be there to transport me to my hotel when I have completed a walk. Also, I agonize over problems that might arise with public transportation: a misread or obsolete schedule, a strike, acts of a supreme deity, etc. If you do not cherish the thought of being marooned at walk's end, leave your car at your destination.

Part Two

35 Great Walks

How to Use the Thirty-Five Walk Descriptions

Each walk is organized into the following information:

1. **Key to Symbols**: One or more of the following symbols will be found at the beginning of each walk description to give you an idea of what to expect to see along the way:

Abbey/Cathedral

Coast/Beach/Lake

Cliffs

Castle

Cable Car

Mountains

Villa/Palace

River

Forest

Art/Museum

2. The **General Description** is a short compendium of the topography and historical sites that you will encounter along the route. No attempt has been made to be comprehensive, and it is suggested that you consult the guidebooks mentioned earlier and other sources for more comprehensive historical information.

3. The **Optional Maps** section provides you with maps that may make your walking experience more interesting, especially if you enjoy working with a topographical map or desire to expand your walking adventures in a particular area. Many of the maps mentioned in this section can be purchased at bookstores in the general area of the walk described. However, as you venture farther into the hinterland availability becomes less certain. To be assured of a desired map, make your purchases in Dublin or Belfast. In any case, all of the walks have been designed to preclude the necessity of optional maps.

4. The **Time/Distance** section includes the length of time necessary to complete the walk at a rate of about 2.5 miles to 3 miles (4 to 5 kilometers) per hour and the distance in miles and kilometers.

5. The location of **Toilet Facilities** along the trail has been included. Often, however, there are none, which is why information has also been included on the amount of privacy. In general, men should have little trouble relieving themselves anywhere along the trail. On trails where much privacy has been indicated, women should also have no problems. Even where a trail is noted as having less than much privacy, women will usually have a number of suitable opportunities. Also, remember that you can usually use rest rooms at bars, restaurants, and train stations.

6. Where you can obtain **Refreshments**, either at a restaurant, cafe, or bar has also been noted. However, do not neglect to bring water with you on any walk.

7. Instructions on how to arrive at the starting point via automobile and public transportation have been included in the **Getting There** section.

8. The **Trail Notes** correspond to the map, and indicate the general course of the trail. They have been structured so that they may be marked with a check after corresponding landmarks have been achieved. Although the inclusion of a note does not necessarily indicate a problem, notes have been provided wherever problems exist. In any case, always watch for waymarks (when they exist) and study your map.

9. At the end of each section, some **Suggestions For More Walking** have been included. Wherever possible, other day walks have been included as well as possibilities for shortening or extending each of the 35 selected walks.

Walk 1: Carlingford

Walk: A Walk along the Tain Trail

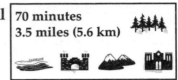

70 minutes
3.5 miles (5.6 km)

General Description

A good stop between Dublin and Belfast.

Peopled by a few hundred people, rocky shored Omeath still looks and acts like a fishing village but is slowly gaining popularity as a resort. Along the blink-your-eyes-and-you-missed-it main street, there are a few shops, restaurants, and pubs, but little in the way of accommodation (only a youth hostel). However, this highly scenic, short-streeted town is known for its fresh seafood. Lunch or dinner, a pint or two of Guinness, and a stroll around town form the perfect ending to a great first walk in this green-valley paradise.

The trail begins just outside of Omeath where the climb onto Carlingford Mountain is initially breathtaking, but soon becomes a gentle slope allowing for breath catching and view scanning. As the trail levels, you will follow a crumbling stone fence and enjoy excellent views through the voluminous blooming deciduous forest of the Mourne Mountains and the rippling waters of the lake. In an afternoon of panoramic views, the best are at walk's end as you descend steeply from Carlingford Mountain and survey from a lofty perch both Carlingford and Carlingford Lough—a grand climax to an all Carlingford sort of day.

Currently a resort, Carlingford finds its origin in the darkness of the Middle Ages when blood thirsty, horned-helmeted Vikings terrorized the otherwise placid Irish countryside. Centuries later, victorious Normans killed their way across England and settled the area. Serenely situated on the placid shore of Carlingford Lough, the town is a delightful relic of the Irish Middle Ages with its crumbling castle, thought provoking abbey, and other remnants of an epoch almost completely buried in the sands of time. The harbor area is home to the main medieval historical sights, most notably the crumbling twelfth-century King John's Castle, which looms over the north side of the harbor and cries out in its gray eminence for regal restoration. Other medieval sites include the fifteenth-century Taafe's Castle, which is currently in private hands, the fortified house known as the Mint, which stands near the town square and was perhaps used as (surprise!) a mint, a three-story gateway that spans the main street, and the ruins of a Dominican Friary at the south end of town.

Optional Maps/Topo-Guides: O.S. Discovery Series Map #29, although no map is necessary

Time/Distance: 1 hour 10 minutes/3.5 miles (5.6 kilometers); add an extra 30 minutes if you start at Omeath

Difficulties: An initial three-minute climb followed by about twenty minutes of gentle ascending

Toilet Facilities: None between towns, but much privacy

Refreshments: Bars and restaurants at both towns

Getting There: From Carlingford, several buses per day pass through Omeath. However, if you take the bus to Omeath, you will have to walk out along the road for about a mile (1.6 kilometers) before you get to the trail head. A better alternative, unless you are compelled by inner demons to visit wide-spot-in-the-road Omeath, is to ask the bus driver to drop you at the trail head. Be certain to specify that you wish to get off at the first brown sign that indicates the Tain Trail. Be vigilant yourself; this sign is not easy to see, but note that it comes shortly after a white and black sign that has a picnic table and a tree on it. If you get off at the second Tain Trail sign, you will realize the error because you will be walking away from Carlingford.

Trail Notes

___ 1. From the trail head, you will ascend a double tracked, partially grassy path, and then a minute or so later you will come to a fork where you will go left on a grassy path (you will see a yellow arrow). From this point, just follow the arrows.
___ 2. About an hour from the trail head, watch for an arrow pointing left. There is a house here with yellow bricks and you will see Carlingford below.

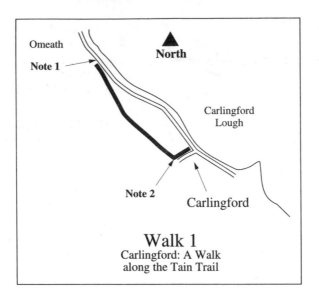

Walk 1
Carlingford: A Walk
along the Tain Trail

Suggestions for More Walking

The Tain Trail cuts a circular, 25-mile (40-kilometer) path around the Cooley Peninsula. Although there is little public transportation, except in the portion described above, it is possible for distance walkers to cover the route in two days by leaving a car at Ravensdale, walking to Carlingford to spend the night, and finishing the walk the next day at Ravensdale.

Walk 2: Belfast/Bangor

Walk: Helen's Bay to Bangor

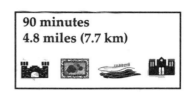

90 minutes
4.8 miles (7.7 km)

General Description

While not entirely a media construct, Belfast's fearsome reputation is not usually deserved. There is no doubt that you will want to avoid this city during periods when the troubles result in open violence, but peace is currently the primary state of being in this lively city. However, I would suggest that you stay tuned to the BBC as you approach Belfast (and other major centers in Northern Ireland); the troubles are well documented on both radio and television and the immediacy of the sights and sounds of a nation in crisis will be your warning to skip Belfast and sojourn in Bangor.

While strolling about downtown Belfast and the University district, you will be scarcely aware of the violence that has racked this city on many occasions—no barbed wire, little or no military presence, and no bombed out buildings. Busy port and capital of Northern Ireland since 1920, central Belfast retains a mostly Victorian aspect. However, the industry that was the basis of the nineteenth-century wealth of Belfast is still evident—docks, decaying factories, and miles of impoverished rowhouses surround the prosperity of the city center. At city center, you will want to visit the Renaissance-style City Hall which was built around the turn of the century. A guided tour will take you about this elaborately (actually ostentatiously) decorated but interesting structure where you will discover the history of Belfast through stained glass windows and a stunning mural. The City Hall is surrounded by the geographic hub of Belfast, Donegall Square, where you will want to stroll through the effusive gardens (horticulturists and other fans of flora will also wish to visit the Botanic Gardens in the University district) and proceed up to St. Anne's Cathedral, which was begun in 1899 but not finished until 1981—almost as long as it takes to have a kitchen remodeled in my neighborhood. The Ulster Museum, the national museum, and art gallery of Northern Ireland, which includes fine arts and crafts from primarily Irish sources, also merits a visit. Finally, pub crawlers will want to imbibe at the intricately decorated Victorian-era Crown Liquor Saloon, which is now owned and operated by the National Trust. If you are contemplating a sojourn of more than a couple days, consult the tourist office for more obscure local sights.

Passing from urban Belfast to rural obscurity, you will hop gingerly from the iron horse, quickly course along a forested trail, almost immediately pass under two ornate bridges whose medieval appearance belies their early twentieth-century origin, and arrive at scenic Helen's Bay where there is nothing to do but stare in rapt disbelief at the turgid, tormented sea and begin the trek back to Bangor. This trail is basically a heavily used recreational band between Belfast and Bangor which is extremely popular with pudgy Northern Irelanders who, on a sunny day, cover every grain of sand with their lobster-red corpulence—not a tan for miles around, only the heartbreak and pain of blazing scarlet-hued skin. Dermatologists who specialize in damaged skin should consider relocating to this area. The rest of the way into Bangor involves trekking from beach to beach, passing an occasional World War II bunker while enjoying extended views of green hills to your right. As you reach Bangor, opulent mansions tower over the bay and quite appropriately, given the opulent neighborhood, you will pass an expansive, amazingly well-groomed golf course.

Bangor is a many-masted, attractive port city that now caters mainly to families, retirees, and a growing bedroom community of former Belfast residents who like life in the slow lane but covet a quick commute to Belfast for work. In spite of Bangor's increasingly geriatric presence, a lively atmosphere prevails. Children, in particular, will delight in the amusement park ambience—games, rides (try the floating-swan for a unique experience), cheap souvenir shops, etc. Although lovely in aspect, Bangor houses few sights of any significance. However, you may wish to visit Bangor Castle which houses the town hall and the Heritage Center which traces, in detail from prehistoric times, the history of Bangor. If you have time for a short excursion, visit the Ulster Folk and Transport Museum about five miles west of Bangor. This living museum includes a variety of vintage structures inhabited during park hours by traditionally clad hosts who recreate the lives of their long dead and hopefully departed ancestors.

Optional Maps/Topo-Guides: O.S. Discovery Series Map #15

Time/Distance: 1 hour 30 minutes / 4.8 miles (7.7 kilometers), although no map is necessary

Difficulties: None

Toilet Facilities: Only at the Helen's Bay beach and Bangor; little privacy on a clear day, otherwise some privacy

Refreshments: Refreshments at Helen's Bay beach; restaurants, bars, and stores at Bangor

Getting There: Take one of the numerous trains from Bangor to Helen's Bay; alternately, if you are staying in Belfast, take the train to Helen's Bay and then return to Belfast from Bangor. To exit the train, you will note instructions to "push in and pull down" on the door. This deft maneuver did not work for me, so I cleverly reached outside and turned the exterior handle—barely escaping before the train departed the platform.

Trail Notes

___ 1. Walk to the end of the platform in the same direction that the train continues. You will descend on a covered staircase, walk along a dirt path for a couple minutes, and then turn right at the first trail which will take you under the train tracks.
___ 2. When you arrive at the beach parking lot seven or eight minutes later, you will continue straight ahead to the coast; you will see a sign indicating "Helen's Bay Beach/Crawfordsburn Country Park."
___ 3. When you reach the coast, go right along the path that parallels the beach.
___ 4. In Bangor, watch for Main Street (currently, there is a Kentucky Fried Chicken franchise on the corner) where you will turn right and ascend to the train station.

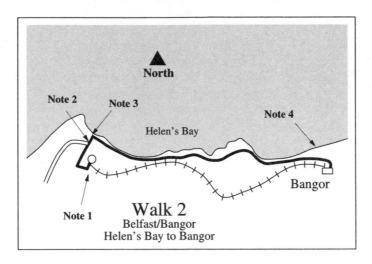

Suggestions for More Walking

This walk can be extended to ten miles (16 kilometers) by taking the train to Hollywood or shortened by taking the train to one of the nearer train stations.

Walk 3: Antrim Village Walk

Walk: **Waterfoot (Glenariff) to Cushendun via the Ulster Way**

110 minutes
5.8 miles (9.3 km)

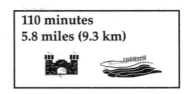

General Description

Driving north along the North Channel coast from Belfast to the Giant's Causeway, you will roll through some of Northern Ireland's finest seaside scenery and a comely collection of remote villages (this area, perhaps the least influenced by English conquerors, did not have an all-weather coach road until the 1830s). The villages are situated at the termini of a group of nine lovely valleys known as the Antrim Glens. Hasten not through the seventy miles (112 kilometers) between Larne and Ballycastle. Savor the views of hill and dale; gaze longingly into the crashing waves of the ocean; and explore infinitely tiny, but warmly embracing, villages.

Beginning in Waterfoot at the edge of a steeply descending glen, today's walk takes you through three of Antrim's finest villages. Waterfoot, a comely collection of bars, restaurants, shops, cottages, etc. assembled along a single street, resides tranquilly in one of Antrim's most memorable valleys (A glen is a valley, and the town Waterfoot is frequently called Glenariff because of its location in Glenariff. I am not sure if this information is worth much, but it certainly will give those with the inclination to philosophize about the nature of identity something to ponder).

Ascending from Waterfoot, you will realize that even picture-perfect Ireland is not without blemish: local trash (not the human type; your security is not threatened) is strewn along a short section of an otherwise lovely walk. Quickly kicking your way through the trash and continuing along the path to Cushendun, you will be rewarded by excellent views of Waterfoot and its harbor. Not far from Waterfoot, you will pass the disintegrating remains of Red Arch Castle poised powerfully above the bay; and, approaching Cushendall, you will skirt a trailer park and be given a view of the Irish as they go about their business far from the peering eyes of most travelers. Winsome Cushendall, a lovely short stop along the way, harbors but a single small sight, the early nineteenth- century red watch tower known as the Curfew Tower (although my observations indicate that there is and could have been no place to go and, therefore, no need for a Curfew Tower).

On the initial trek out of Cushendall, you will pass a series of fine homes constructed in a variety of styles, all with magnificent views. You will also pass Layd Church which is currently in ruin but worth a short detour. Passing from the confines of Cushendall, you will leave civilization behind and embark upon a rustic passage amid farms, farmhouses, farm animals and abandoned farm buildings—even farm fans will be farmed out. Farmland eventually cedes to forest, and the route becomes frequently alpine in appearance.

Your ultimate destination, Cushendun, is an indescribable haven of tranquility—a truly beautiful place along the banks of the North

Channel and justifiably registered with the National Trust. Cushendun's fifty or so inhabitants live a highly privileged existence in the penumbra of not too shadowy past as they wander about in a lovely whitewashed quasi-Georgian architectural environment. (If the theory of architectural determinism—that people's behavior is deeply influenced by the structures they inhabit and the general ambience of these structures—is true, then the inhabitants of Cushendun must be among the finest beings to trod this often cursed planet.) As you stroll about the town, peer above the roofs and into the luxuriously verdant hills serenely subdivided by antique stone fences forming a pattern worthy of many yards of canvas.

Optional Maps/Topo-Guides: O.S. Discovery Series Map #5 (Ballycastle)

Time/Distance: 1 hour 50 minutes / 5.8 miles (9.3 kilometers)

Difficulties: There is a 35 minute, gradual climb out of Cushendall

Toilet Facilities: At all three towns

Refreshments: Restaurants and bars in Waterfoot and Cushendall; tea house in Cushendun

Getting There: Five buses (#162) per day make the trip between Cushendun and Waterfoot. For current scheduling information call Ulster Bus at Larne (01574) 272345.

Trail Notes

___ 1. From the bus stop in Waterfoot, walk back on the road in the direction that the bus arrived from.
___ 2. Turn right at the main road; you will see an Ulster Way sign.
___ 3. After a few minutes, you will go left and ascend on a narrow asphalt path.
___ 4. When you reach the main road (shortly after passing a school), go left and follow the road as it curves and goes over a river into the downtown area. When you get to the main intersection, you will go right (there is a sign indicating "Golf Course" and "Youth Hostel").
___ 5. When you reach a fork, just beyond the town, you will go to

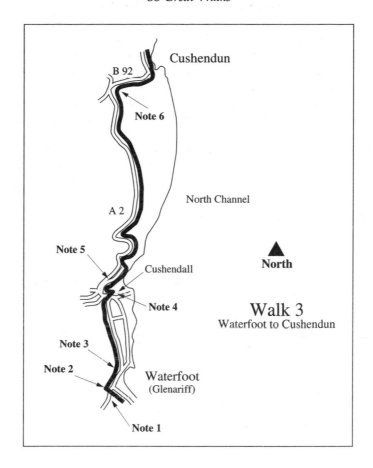

Cushendun

B 92

Note 6

North Channel

A 2

Note 5

Cushendall

Note 4

▲
North

Walk 3
Waterfoot to Cushendun

Note 3

Note 2

Waterfoot
(Glenariff)

Note 1

your right (although both routes eventually take you to the same place, the right fork is more picturesque) where you will eventually see a marker indicating "Cliff Walk." You will eventually join the other road either at the youth hostel or past the ruins of the Layd Church; in either case, turn right on the asphalt road.

___ 6. Just past the St. Ciaran's school, you will turn right on a main road (B 92) that will take you to Cushendun in about fifteen minutes (you will pass the Glens of Antrim Residential and Private Nursing Home—tired walkers may wish to check in for a few days).

Suggestions for More Walking

This walk can be shortened by taking the bus to Cushendall. According to official sources, this section of the Ulster Way extends down to Larne (also on this bus route) but the route is not marked on O.S. Discovery Series map #9; you could, however, follow some of the secondary roads north from Larne or another point if you are going to be in the area for a while. Also see Walks 4 and 5 below.

Walk 4: Giant's Causeway

Walk: Dunseverick Castle to Giant's Causeway

General Description

100 minutes	
5 miles (8 km)	

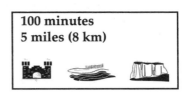

Although "castle," the word, may conjure images of towering towers and crafty crenulations—expect not Disneyland. Today's walk begins at a very special place, the crumbling remains of Dunseverick Castle, which is in danger of disappearing completely. You may be one of the final visitors to what remains of a castle keep that during the Middle Ages stood as a sentinel against foreign agression. This is an opportune moment to commune with the loneliness and fear that characterized the European Middle Ages—imagine yourself huddled in the damp, drafty keep while peering into the distance at a real or imagined juggernaut hurtling headlong in your direction, and your phone is out of order. The Terror, The Terror.

Departing Dunseverick with vivid images of medieval times still darting about your mind, you will almost immediately join one of the most stunning coastal paths in Ireland—towering cliffs, crashing waves, rugged shoals, and deep views into the immensity of the Atlantic Ocean are your constant companions. Cackling sea gulls dive nearby while mocking the walking for such a slow, inefficient mode of transport.

Astonishing views become surreal vistas of the sea and rocky off-shore islands as you approach the Giant's Causeway. Occasionally shifting focus from the far to the near, you will delight in the lovely effusions of wild flowers which hang precariously from rocky cliffs in seeming defiance of gravity and rejoice in a comely collection of iridescent butterflies flitting about the trail.

Northern Ireland's most popular tourist attraction, Giant's Causeway billed as the eighth wonder of the world, was formed from a volcanic eruption about sixty million years ago. As flowing lava cooled, it formed remarkable columns—mostly hexagonal in shape—that extend from the cliffs far into the sea. This is truly a remarkable sight and an excellent opportunity for you to mill about, shoulder to shoulder, with other slackjawed rock gawkers.

Optional Maps/Topo-Guides: Both O.S. Discovery Series Maps #4 and #5 show the course of this route, although you cannot get lost. There is also a useful walking brochure available at the park office.

Time/Distance: 1 hour 40 minutes / 5 miles (8 kilometers)

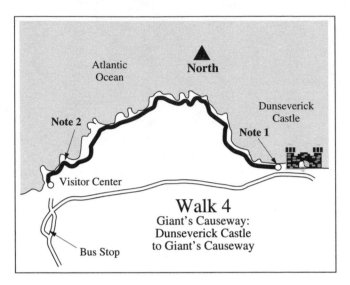

Atlantic
Ocean

North

Dunseverick
Castle

Note 2

Note 1

Visitor Center

Walk 4
Giant's Causeway:
Dunseverick Castle
to Giant's Causeway

Bus Stop

Difficulties: Numerous, minor ups and downs

Toilet Facilities: Only at the Giant's Causeway tourist center; much privacy

Refreshments: Only at the Giant's Causeway tourist center

Getting There: Six buses daily (four on Saturday, none Sunday) link Giant's Causeway with Dunseverick Castle. The bus stop is along the road just outside of the tourist center. Make sure the bus driver is completely aware of your need to descend at Dunseverick Castle and watch yourself for a crumbling castle keep (all that remains of this soon to disappear monument) where the road comes close to the sea.

Trail Notes

___ 1. From the small parking lot where the bus stops, you will follow a stairway leading down to the coastal path.

___ 2. After about 1 hour and 25 minutes, you will descend along a deep stone stairway to the spectacle of the Giant's Causeway. From here you may take one of the frequent buses back to the tourist center or walk back to the center along the asphalt path.

Suggestions for More Walking

For an extra two miles (3.2 kilometers), take the bus to White Park Bay; or for an extra four miles (6.4 kilometers), ride out to Ballintoy. Another proximate possibility is to take the ferry to quiet Rathlin Island just off the coast of Ballycastle where you can explore for several hours while waiting for the infrequent ferry to return you to the mainland. The tourist office (tel. 62024) on Ballycastle's coast can provide you with scheduling information. Also see Walk 5 below.

Walk 5: Antrim Resort Coast

Walk: Portrush to Portstewart

General Description

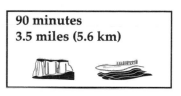

90 minutes
3.5 miles (5.6 km)

Both of today's beach towns attract hordes of tourists during July and August but are otherwise fairly quiet. Larger Portrush has a more carnival-like, youthful atmosphere, while more stately Portstewart caters to a slightly more staid clientele. You will not be rubbing the shoulders of too many international tourists in these towns, which provide an opportunity to experience an unspoiled Irish holiday.

Portrush with its two beaches and sometimes riotous atmosphere is a popular summer destination for many Irish families. If you enjoy beach life, amusement-park rides, arcades, and the bar scene, you will delight in a short summer sojourn. Otherwise there is not much to see and an overnight stay coupled with today's friendly beach walk will suffice.

The trek to Portstewart begins with an engaging stroll through Portrush's colorful town center and then proceeds along a lovely, sandy beach that is quite underused given the usually cool weather in Ulster.

Leaving the beach behind, you will continue along a lonely rock strewn coast that hosts only a few intrepid fishermen boldly standing about slippery shoals with net and rod, contemplating tonight's dining experience. One rocky, wave-crashing cove after another comes to view in a very short period of time, and soon you will arrive at the grave of the unknown sailor who must have washed up on the shore lifeless and without identification. Although often gray, the day will be brightened by ubiquitous seagulls and a colorful assortment of wildflowers. Just outside of Portstewart there is a promontory, literally and figuratively a high point in the walk, where you will savor views of both towns rising from their respective banks.

Also crowded during the summer, Portstewart caters to a more sedate multitude. Again, there is not much to see but the nautical atmosphere, including a few wet-suited, die-hard surfers, which gives this town an off-beat atmosphere that will be perhaps more inviting to adult travelers than the more family-like atmosphere at Portrush.

Optional Maps/Topo-Guides: O.S. Discovery Series Map #4

Time/Distance: 1 hour 15 minutes / 3.5 miles (5.6 kilometers)

Difficulties: Numerous minor ups and downs

Toilet Facilities: At both towns; occasional privacy

Refreshments: At both towns

Getting There: From the bus stop at Portstewart town center take the bus back to Portrush.

Trail Notes

___ 1. From the bus stop at Portrush, head directly into town on Dunluce Ave. Continue along this road for a couple of minutes until you see the amusement park rides. Directly in front of these rides is the beach. Make your way down to the beach and walk left on the asphalt promenade that parallels the beach.

___ 2. At the end of the promenade, ascend on the narrow asphalt path

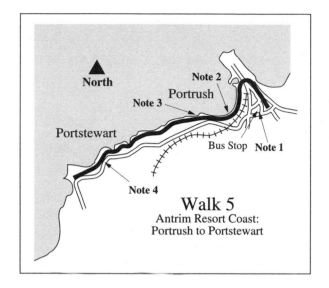

North

Note 2

Note 3 Portrush

Portstewart

Bus Stop **Note 1**

Note 4

Walk 5
Antrim Resort Coast:
Portrush to Portstewart

that leads to the main road where you will turn right.

___ 3. Continue along the main road for a couple minutes, and then turn right toward the coast where you will see the sign indicating the "Ulster Way"; when you reach the coast, go left on the well worn path that skirts the cliffs and forms the edge of a golf course.

___ 4. About midway through the second golf course, you will be forced from the coast and up to the sidewalk that parallels the main road for the last fifteen minutes of today's walk.

Suggestions for More Walking

The 3.5-mile (5.6-kilometer) walk from Dunluce Castle, east of Portrush, to Portrush is pleasant, but involves about a mile of roadwalking (along a sidewalk) before reaching the extensive beach that leads to Portrush. Also problematic is the lack of regular transportation; only one late-afternoon bus per day connects the two points. Also see Walks 3 and 5. Dunluce to Portrush; See Walk 3 above.

Walk 6: Glenveagh National Park

Walk: A Ramble from Glenveagh Castle

General Description

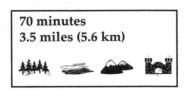

70 minutes
3.5 miles (5.6 km)

Glenveagh National Park, situated in a lovely, barely populated (except for millions of sheep) region, is reminiscent of the Scottish Highlands—lakes, mountains, and fog everywhere. John Adair found it attractive enough to callously evict small landholders during the mid-nineteenth century in order to consolidate his massive estate which was sold to the Irish National Trust in the 1970s. The main attractions are the castle and its surrounding gardens. The relatively new, nineteenth-century castle appears to be a relic of the Middle Ages with its cyclopean walls and threatening turrets. Inside, however, the castle exudes a commodious Victorian warmth. Although I do not always enthuse during castle tours, the tour of Glenveagh Castle is not to be missed; it will take you into the lives of the nineteenth-and early-twentieth-century privileged elite. Charlie Chaplin, Greta Garbo and other luminaries have sojourned in this environment of unparalleled comfort and sumptuousness that eludes, and continues to elude, the masses of Irish. Antique afficianados will delight in the superb collection of fine furniture that still graces the rooms of the castle.

Encircling the castle is one of Ireland's most attractive gardens which was begun in the nineteenth century and continually expanded and refined over the decades. Tearing yourself from this rich botanical display, you will walk away from the masses and delight in a private back-to-nature experience reserved only for the independent walker. Today, you will penetrate an ancient oak forest while skirting the banks of lovely Lough Beagh. This is a totally satisfying and ethereal experience as clouds swirl about mysteriously and serrated peaks rise precipitously from the mist in grizzled eminence over Lough Beagh's far shore. Continuing to make your way through the quiet forest, you will dodge the large, moss-covered boulders that are strewn about the lake shore. The walk back presents substantially different vistas and the bonus of having the castle in view most of the time.

Optional Maps: Included with your admission to the park is an excellent topographical map; also O.S. Discovery Series Map #6

Time/Distance: 1 hour 10 minutes / 3.5 miles (5.6 kilometers) to and from lake's end

Difficulties: None

Toilet Facilities: At the castle and visitor center; some privacy

Refreshments: At the castle and visitor center

Getting There: Take the shuttle bus from the visitor center to the castle.

Trail Notes

___ 1. From the bus stop at Glenveagh Castle, walk through the tourist office to the other side and follow the path to your right down to the lake where you turn left. Continue along the shore avoiding the climb to your left.

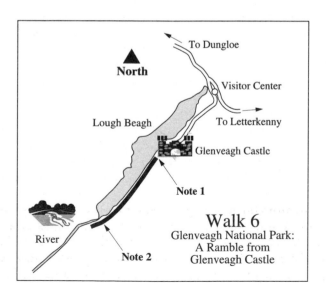

___ 2. At lake's end you may retrace your steps to the castle or continue along as far as you wish.

Suggestions for More Walking

This walk can be shortened by simply turning around at any point, or lengthened by following the river for some distance. You can also create a very long circular ramble back to the castle by connecting the river trail with some of the side roads shown on the map you will receive at the park entrance.

Walk 7: Ulster-American Folk Park/Gortin History Park

Walk: Gortin to the Gortin History Park

General Description

70 minutes
3.5 miles (5.6 km)

Gortin is a one-street town—a nice street that has a complement of the requisite watering holes and shops, all neatly arranged and pleasing to the eye. However, beyond relaxing and imbibing at this scenic locale, there is nothing to keep you from a quick departure.

The ramble out of Gortin skirts a spindly but hyper-quick stream of pure Irish water that will make you want to leap in headlong clutching a bar of Irish Spring soap for a refreshing wallow. You will probably, however, skip this option in favor of continuing along the trail where you will be reverently awed by the gift of great beauty that has been endowed to this verdant valley—a silvery stream, abundantly blooming flora, multi-hued birds flitting about everywhere, and placid sheep grazing contentedly on grass that no one need mow. If you seek bucolic serenity at its most rustic—seek no farther.

In contrast to the splendid rusticity of this walk's inception, the second leg of the journey has an almost ominous appearance, particularly on a cloudy day. Much local timber has been harvested and the result seems to be an aura of threatening isolation as the remaining trees appear poised to hasten—roots, branches, and all—down the hill after their human persecutors who tread thoughtlessly through the offended forest. However, the views into the distant hills are superb and almost compensate for the numbing awareness of the tree terror that we all harbor deep within our collective angst. Less confident walkers will whistle as if gingerly circumambulating a dark cemetery along this stretch.

Approaching the park, you will cruise through a leafy green tunnel of healthy, amicable trees that will help to allay your tree terror and restore certitude in the benevolence of objects that extend loftily from the earth's surface. Finally, just before the park, vigilantly watch for the concrete bench that sagely advises in solemnly carved letters "REST AND BE THANKFUL"—practical wisdom to abide by in our daily lives.

The Gortin History Park, today's walk's terminus, is not the primary attraction in this area but it is a worthy stop on your way to the Ulster-American Folk Park. The Gortin History Park exhibitions trace human habitation in Ireland from earliest times through the seventeenth century. The full-scale replicas of mesolithic and neolithic encampments serve as reminders of the incredible discomfort associated with human existence until very recent times, while the Norman Motte and Bailey are reminiscent of not only discomfort but fear and the need for self defense that permeates our lives. A variety of other exhibits realistically portray the hardships associated with early life in Ireland.

The nearby Ulster-American Folk Park (not on the trail but one of my favorite Irish attractions) portrays realistically the story of eighteenth-century Irish emigrants to America. Your journey through the park begins at a typical Ulster Village. The structures are authentic and include the home of American tycoon Thomas Mellon who emigrated from Northern Ireland in the early nineteenth century. Passing from the village, you will find yourself waiting for passage to America along a dock with a backdrop of dreary brick buildings, a stark contrast to the American-streets-paved-in-gold image that captured the imagination of many emigrants. The emigrants' lives did not improve on board where you will tour the densely packed living quarters to the accompaniment of genuine imitation nautical sounds and nautical motion.

In contrast to emigrants who rocked and rolled for several nausea-inducing weeks, you will land in America after only a few minutes and find yourself wandering about a pre-combustion-engine American town. Your ultimate destination is a Pennsylvania village, where you would theoretically settle if you were a genuine Irish immigrant. This is truly a fascinating experience which is enhanced by the numerous guides in period costume who practice crafts and aid the bewildered visitor.

Optional Maps: O.S. Discovery Series Map #13

Time/Distance: 1 hour 15 minutes / 3.5 miles (5.6 kilometers)

Difficulties: A substantial amount of moderate climbing

Toilet Facilities: At both Gortin and the Gortin History Park; some privacy

Refreshments: At both Gortin and the Gortin History Park

Getting There: The Gortin History park is about seven miles (11.2 kilometers) north of Omagh. Several buses per day pass the park from Omagh on the way to Gortin. Wait in front of the park by the telephone booth and wave the driver down. Schedules are available at the tourist office and bus station in Omagh.

Trail Notes

___ 1. Emerging from the bus, you will cross the street and walk in the direction that the bus continues until you traverse a small bridge over a stream. Turn right along the path that is clearly marked by a sign along the path.
___ 2. When you join the main road about 25 minutes later, continue straight in the direction of Omagh. In a couple minutes, you will see a direction post with a hiker that indicates "Ulster Way" (you also see a large sign indicating "Gortin Glen Park") leading you to the right and away from the main road. Continue to follow the wide double-track path, avoiding the temptation to go left

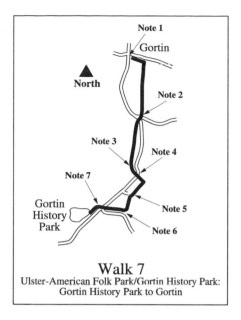

Walk 7
Ulster-American Folk Park/Gortin History Park:
Gortin History Park to Gortin

on a dirt path. You will soon see an arrow pointing in your direction.

___ 3a. About 40 minutes into the walk, you are climbing steeply and you will see a crest. Currently there are several markers pointing left, but they are stapled on to trees and tree parts (i.e. they may disappear). Watch carefully for this turn which leads onto a gravel path that is about the same width as the one that you are on. Soon you will see a permanent post with an arrow.

___ 3b. Watch carefully for a narrow path that goes left; this turn is clearly marked and leads into the deep forest, but you must watch for it.

___ 3c. Watch for another marker in a clearing about 50 meters ahead.

___ 4a. When you reach the road, you will cross the fence over a couple stairs.

___ 4b. Cross the road and go right and climb another couple stairs to continue away from the main road on a wide path. There is an arrow pointing you in the correct direction.

___ 5. When the first opportunity to join the main road occurs, just continue along the path.

___ 6. When you reach a dead end at an asphalt road, go to your right (you will signs for the Ulster Way leading you left, but this route will not take you back to the history park).

___ 7. When you reach the main road, turn left and continue down to the history park. (Soon you will see a trail on your left that parallels the main road; you may follow this route back to the small house that is the park office and then turn right to reach the road.)

Suggestions for More Walking

It is possible to continue from the Gortin History Park to Ulster-American Folk Park via a series of back roads that lead to a bridge over the Strule River. O.S. Discovery Series Map #12 will help you plan a route. However, I would not attempt this walk without first scouting your way in a motor vehicle—you could become lost for days, if not longer in the maze of asphalt strips that criss-cross the area. If you attempt this puzzle, and are successful, you can take a bus back to Omagh from the Ulster-American Folk Park. If you are not successful, a bus will not be necessary.

Walk 8: Lough Derg/Station Island

Walk: Pettigo to Station Island via the Pilgrims' Route

| 90 minutes |
| 4.9 miles (7.8 km) |

General Description

Pettigo is an elfin collection of shops and homes catering mainly to pilgrims who occasionally stop for a meal or bed on their way to sleepless starvation. The tourist office/local bakery dishes up helpful information as well as sumptuous scones in two savory flavors, and if you are not taking the pilgrimage boat out to the island, you may enjoy the quick, painless, and informative "Lough Derg Journey" at the visitor center.

You will part from the town along a main road (main for this barely inhabited region), but soon the trail departs from the world of

vehicular traffic and becomes quite comely—a flowery, leafy haven with excellent views of the surrounding hills. You will also pass a number of rough- hewn, stone farm structures probably uninhabited since the notorious Potato Famine, long past rigor mortis, and tumbling into final decay. Watch for the tiny lake where sheep graze gracefully while pondering the joy of a long cool quaff of pure limpid liquid, and if you have the extra time, take the ten minute (each way) detour to the Carn Graveyard, which has chillingly arranged grave stones that invoke irrational fear especially on a stormy day. Dating back to the seventeenth century, this necropolis was sometimes visited and occasionally inhabited by pilgrims. However, if you have no deep desire to commune with the dead today, you may pass gingerly by to purgatory.

Emblazoned over the entrance to Station Island's parking lot is the ominous sign "Saint Patrick's Purgatory." It is astonishing that so many well warned people would so freely enter a world that the word "purgatory" is used to describe. Would anyone vacation at a Caribbean resort designated Purgatory Isle? Spin doctors, your services are needed here. You cannot visit the island (one of Ireland's most important pilgrimage sites) as a simple tourist; you must be a participant in an actual pilgrimage which means three days of torture and penance during the busy months of July and August. Pilgrims doff their shoes for a continuous circumambulation of the island and foreswear the joys of food as atonement for their sins. Those accustomed to less rigorous suffering and not shamed by slacker status can go as a day tripper during the spring or fall. The island closes during the winter.

Even if you do not participate in a pilgrimage, Station Island is a magnificent, if not foreboding, sight completely blanketed with solemn, gray-stone buildings, which fade almost imperceptibly into a dense, gray mist on an overcast day. You may also take a boat ride around this lovely valley lake, which has several other tiny, uninhabited islands and is surrounded by a succession of gently inclined, stony faced slopes.

Optional Maps: O.S. Discovery Series Map #11

Time/Distance: 1 hour 30 minutes / 4.9 miles (7.8 kilometers)

Difficulties: Several minor ups and downs

Toilet Facilities: At Pettigo and the parking lot at Lough Derg; some privacy

Refreshments: Bars, restaurants, and stores at Pettigo

Getting There: From the parking lot at Lough Derg, currently two buses per day return to Pettigo in the afternoon. The staff at the ferry office can call a taxi which is moderately priced for this short ride (you can also reserve a taxi at the tourist office).

Trail Notes

___ 1. From the town center at Pettigo, walk down the narrow asphalt road that leads to Lough Derg. You will pass several B&Bs, but if you are in doubt, ask anyone to help.

___ 2. When you come to a fork a few minutes later, go left on a nameless asphalt road and ignore the "Lough Derg" sign that takes

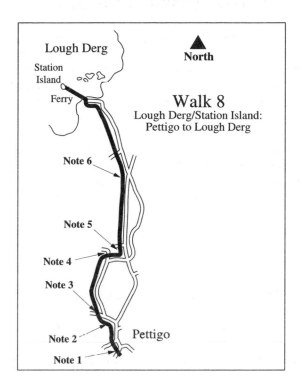

Lough Derg

Station
Island

Ferry

▲
North

Walk 8
Lough Derg/Station Island:
Pettigo to Lough Derg

Note 6

Note 5

Note 4

Note 3

Note 2

Note 1

Pettigo

you to the right.
___ 3. When you come to the next fork, go right.
___ 4. About 25 to 30 minutes into the walk, you will turn right onto an asphalt road similar to the one you have been walking along. You will see a post with a red circle and green arrow pointing you in the correct direction.
___ 5. When you reach the main road again, go immediately left where you see the sign indicating "Carn Graveyard." You will also see another post with the red circle and green arrow.
___ 6. About an hour into the walk, you will reach the main road again where you will turn left and follow the road into the parking lot at Lough Derg.

Suggestions for More Walking

You can shorten this walk by starting at any of the main-road junctures seen on the map, and it is possible to lengthen the walk by about one mile (1.6 kilometers) via a visit to the Carn Graveyard. Also, the tourist office can provide you with a brochure describing several interesting walks in the area.

Walk 9: A Moy Valley Excursion in County Mayo

Walk: Killala to Ballina via the Western Way

170 minutes
8.5 miles (13.6 km)

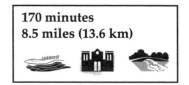

General Description

Killala is a lovely old seaside resort with a prominent Anglican cathedral, inviting imbibing opportunities, and a number of well-kept, quaint shops. This berg's lilliputian proportions belie its historic importance; here, in 1798 the Republic of Ireland was declared and John Moore was named as its first president—impressive events for a blink-your-eyes-and-you-miss-it town.

Stop, have a drink, and walk away from small town Ireland on a long rural trek down the Western Way. Although this is not one of Ireland's great walks, those who enjoy obscure rusticity and have time to burn will have a most pleasant day.

Parting from the main road along a narrow band of asphalt, you will slip under a canopy of green trees and pass a section of homes prior to arriving at abandoned Moyne Abbey which slumbers, almost forgotten along the shores of the River Moy. The abbey was founded in the fifteenth century by Franciscan friars but was pillaged and burned by the English about a century later. Although abandoned by the dawn of the eighteenth century and in an advanced state of decay, enough of Moyne Abbey remains for the imaginative to conjure vividly the spartan existence that characterized the lives of the cloistered. Back on the trail, you will marvel at the views of distant hills and delight in the company of a bevy of beautiful bovines who graze contentedly in Ireland's heifer heaven.

Perched majestically over the Moy River, Rosserk Abbey is well worth the 1.5 mile (2.4 kilometer), round-trip detour. Slightly older than Moyne Abbey, Rosserk was the first Franciscan friary constructed in Ireland. It too was burned by the English is the sixteenth century but is in a better state of preservation than Moyne Abbey. In particular, you will be able to climb a set of stone stairs from the cloisters up to the dormitories that will make today's most austere university dorms appear to be luxury-class accommodations. The ruins do not take long to explore but you will probably wish to linger (perhaps devouring some victuals purchased in Killala) while contemplating the lonely tranquility of medieval Ireland. As an added bonus, you will probably be there alone, since tourist buses cannot negotiate the narrow track that provides Rosserk with its only contact to the outside world. After Rosserk Abbey, the walk is fairly uneventful as you continue along a remote, often stone-walled rural road.

Ballina, attractively situated on the banks of the River Moy, caters to outdoors people, especially fishermen. This is the largest town in North Mayo and there are a variety of accommodations, dining opportunities, and retail options. This is the local bishop's seat, and you may wish to visit the nineteenth-century cathedral, which was built adjacent to the ruins of a fourteenth-century abbey.

Optional Maps: O.S. Discovery Series Map #24

Time/Distance: 2 hours 50 minutes / 8.5 miles (13.6 kilometers)

Difficulties: Several minor ups and downs

Toilet Facilities: None between towns; some privacy

Refreshments: Bars, restaurants, and stores at both towns

Getting There: Two to three buses per day travel from Ballina to Killala (tel. 71800).

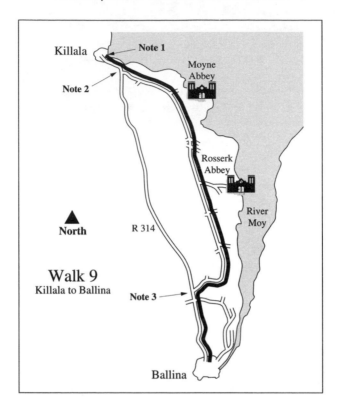

Trail Notes

___ 1. Just walk out along the road that the bus arrived on; you will see the tourist office on your right as you leave town.

___ 2. After about three-quarters of a mile (1.2 kilometers) you will go left at a fork where you see the sign for the Western Way and also a sign indicating "Moyne Abbey." From this point, you will be going almost straight; however, watch for the direction posts at intersections.

___ 3. When you reach the main road, go left and follow it into Ballina about 30 minutes later. Alternately you could take the first unmarked road to the right and follow that into town for an extra half mile (0.75 kilometer).

Suggestions for More Walking

This walk can be shortened by about three-quarters of a mile (1.2 kilometers) by exiting the bus where the trail departs the main road. The Western Way continues through both towns. Buses run to Ballycastle, about seventeen miles (27.2 kilometers) north of Killala, and intersect with the trail about three miles (4.8 kilometers) north of Killala. From Ballina buses do not intersect the trail.

Walk 10: Achill Island

Walk: Cliff Walk

Optional time & distance

General Description

Achill is Ireland's largest island (about 180 square miles/467 square kilometers) and County Mayo's summer playground, attracting hordes of seasonal tourists in search of oceanside frivolity. There are no historic monuments of note on the island so you will have time to enjoy the outside ambience, in particular the expansive beaches and craggy cliffs. The islandscape is almost tropically florid as you cross from the mainland, but becomes increasingly barren and wind-swept as you approach the vicinity of Achill Head. Be careful as you drive about the island; sheep, which seem to easily outnumber people, wander about indiscriminately and appear with disturbing regularity about to wander into traffic.

Although alluring, Keem Beach will sing its siren song in an attempt to seduce you into a slothful afternoon of lounging and swimming, avoid temptation and walk directly up hill away from the crowds where grazing goats will be your only companions. Soon you will begin to trace a path along some of Ireland's most renowned cliffs while marveling at some of this ocean-bound land's most superb views. As you walk in the direction of Achill Head, the views become increasingly spectacular and the beach eventually disappears, leaving you alone in

a world of crashing waves, swirling clouds, vertiginous cliffs. Although it is impossible to reach Achill Head on foot (the cliffs are too steep and the terrain too rugged to support a trail), you will traverse some of Ireland's wildest topography. The trek back is equally spectacular and offers expanding views of what initially appears to be a postage-stamp sized beach that grows as you begin the steep descent from on high. Reaching the beach, you will now have earned the bonus of a good swim and a relaxing repose on the beach.

Optional Maps: O.S. Discovery Series Map #30

Time/Distance: Optional, depending on the distance of the cliff-top walk

Difficulties: Basically a long, difficult climb followed by an equally long descent. Be attentive as you reach the top; the cliffs drop rather abruptly.

Toilet Facilities: At the parking lot

Refreshments: At various small towns along the road to Achill Head

Getting There: Achill Head is at the tip of Achill Island and can be accessed via R319.

Trail Notes

___ 1. At the far end of the parking lot, you will see a narrow, grassy line that seems to project from the rest of the hill. From where you stand, the ascent seems impossible, but once you start climbing the path it becomes clear.

___ 2. As you reach the top, you will see what appears to be a path which goes left or right. Go to the right in the direction of Achill Head (or, if you prefer, turn left to the observation point). Remember this point for the descent. You may, from here, continue as far as you wish or as far as you feel comfortable.

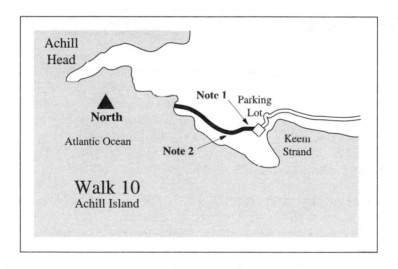

Suggestions for More Walking

You can continue almost all the way to Achill Head. Elsewhere on the island, you can follow some of the side roads or, perhaps, take a trek along lengthy Trawmore Beach.

Walk 11: Westport

Walk: Newport to Westport via the Western Way

165 minutes
8.5 miles (13.6 km)

General Description

Today's walk is a long rural trek between two attractive towns—nothing spectacular but an opportunity to experience Ireland as most Irish know it. You will get a good day's exercise and enjoy a very green, fertile countryside that undulates gracefully if not tediously.

Newport is a quiet spot lingering obscurely along the banks of its eponymous river. Small-town charm abounds here and you will want to spend a few minutes exploring the well-kept shops and cafes lining the single main street or perhaps wander up to the hilltop, pink-granite St. Patrick's Church which was built in the early twentieth century.

Leaving Newport behind, you will enjoy excellent views of the town as you ascend along the river. Soon you will enter rural Ireland and course along a narrow asphalt road often shaded by a tunnel of leafy trees. This bucolic trek traverses vast tracts of cultivated land and is characteristic of the tranquility that permeates County Mayo's farming communities. The final leg of the trek takes you away from the asphalt along a pleasant, grassy path before arriving in lovely Westport.

Westport, a lively up-and-coming town with an attractive collection of Georgian style homes, is pleasantly arrranged along the comely banks of the Carrowbeg River and a central octagon. The facades along Main Street have the appearance of being freshly painted on a daily basis, and all amenities are available. Pub crawlers in particular will enjoy the variety of opportunities to quaff pints of Guinness in a most lively atmosphere. Westport is also a good base for a variety of outdoor activities including horseback riding, fishing, and swimming along nearby sandy beaches.

The main historic sight is Westport House, which was constructed in the eighteenth century by the local English landlord Browne family. You may tour the impressive interior which includes an interesting gallery of family portraits. Outside, you may tour the grounds which house a small zoo, a walled garden, a tacky carnival, and a mini-train.

Optional Maps: O.S. Discovery Series Map #31

Time/Distance: 2 hours 45 minutes / 8.5 miles (13.6 kilometers)

Difficulties: a number of minor ups and downs

Toilet Facilities: None between towns; some privacy

Refreshments: Bars, restaurants, and stores in both towns

Getting There: Two buses per day ply the road from Westport to Newport. Schedules are posted in front of the tourist office in Westport.

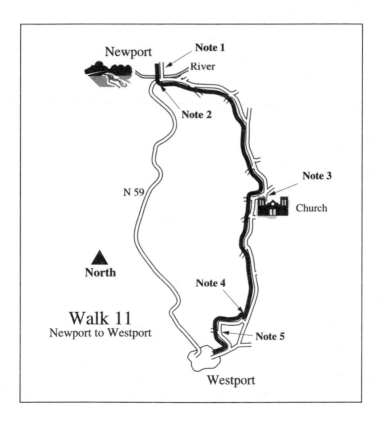

Trail Notes

___ 1. From the center of town, walk back along the main road in the direction that the bus arrived in Newport.

___ 2. After crossing the bridge, go immediately left and up on an asphalt road. You will soon see a post with a yellow arrow and hiker pointing in this direction. From this point, the trail is well marked and you will simply follow the asphalt road without straying down even more obscure paths.

___ 3. When you come to a junction and see a church, go to your right and pass the church.

___ 4. Watch for the post that leads you to a sharp right turn just before you reach the main road. (If you miss this turn, and find yourself at the main road, just turn right and walk into town.) Follow this path as it curves and then makes a sharp left.

___ 5. Go left when you reach a dead end. You will see a house to your right and a factory to your left.

___ 6. When you come to the main road, turn right and you will arrive quickly in town.

Suggestions for More Walking

Although there is no possibility of truncating or extending this walk, you will want to complete Walk 12 on Croagh Patrick while in the area. Also, the Western Way continues through both towns, but there is no possibility of using public transportation to reach a beginning point.

Walk 12: Croagh Patrick

Walk: A Pilgrim's Route to the Sky

120 to 180 minutes

General Description

Croagh Patrick, loftily perched above the Clew Bay, is where, according to legend, St. Patrick (after fasting for 40 days and nights) rang his bell signalling to all the snakes in Ireland that their doom was imminent. Consequently, the snakes plunged en masse to an unpleasant death, and Ireland was forever rid of the feared serpent. Today, Croagh Patrick is a revered pilgrimage site, and thousands of pilgrims climb (some barefooted or on their knees—a remarkable, perhaps lunatic feat of self-mortification) to the summit where there is a small church commemorating this stirring deed. A dark-of-the-night torch walk used to occur on St. Patrick's Day which no doubt produced a mystical sight as thousands of torch-bearing devotees snaked (no pun originally intended, but on second reading I was duly impressed by my unintended cleverness) their way up the mountain.

Beholding the lordly loftiness and abrupt angularity of Croagh Patrick, my first expression was an expletive which I will delete. Although daunted by initial impressions, I dutifully began to trod slowly upward, one step at a time, which leads me to a few words of caution: you will do penance on this extremely rocky and steep trail whether you see the value in such rituals or not. This is evidenced by the numerous walkers overtaken by extreme fatigue who litter the path—watch your step.

Ascending the Croagh, you quickly begin to lose touch with the modern world and begin to psychologically bond with the hundreds of thousands of previous pilgrims who have trod this venerable route. In spite of physical hardships, a series of stunning visual events serves as just emolument. At the trail's inception, a fast-flowing, quicksilver sliver of a stream parallels the trail for a distance imparting the illusion if not the reality of coolness to the tormented walker. Parched sheep with quizzical expressions grudgingly tolerate bipedal intruders while gracefully imbibing at the stream. Gazing into the distance, you will notice that someone has taken the liberty of arranging some of the millions of stones in an aesthetically pleasing arrangement of now crumbling walls that define the mountain's surface at lower elevations. The views of the bay and surrounding terrain become increasingly more powerful as you ascend; and at the summit's base, the views are staggering in all directions. On a clear day especially, the bay poetically reveals its splendorous charms as shades of turquoise and jade blend in a mystical melange of cosmic brilliance, punctuated by sable-colored sand bars and encircled by a ring of earth-toned hills while clouds float wispily about in amorphous artfulness.

Although totally dazzled by the vast tableau and wanting to be further enraptured, I decided to halt the climbing madness just below the final ascent. I had developed a gloomy awareness that my faith was not strong enough for me to claw my way to the precipitous peak and rump slide back to the bottom without tragic or at least debilitating consequences. Good luck if you decide to grapple your way to the summit, but whether you achieve the peak or not, this climb is a most exhilarating experience. The downward trajectory is equally impressive as the remarkable views that were over your shoulder before are now constantly in view.

Not far from Croagh Patrick and worth a quick detour is Murrisk Abbey. Long since abandoned and in an advanced state of decay, this fifteenth-century Augustine abbey lies picturesquely along the coast and invites the discerning visitor to ponder the loneliness of Ireland's Middle Ages.

Optional Maps: O.S. Discovery Series Map #30 and Map #31

Time/Distance: About an hour from the parking lot to the base of the summit and about another hour downhill. Add an extra hour or so if you elect to go to the summit.

Difficulties: This is an almost continuous ascent which requires the walker to go slow—placing one foot in front of another and avoiding large strides. If you are patient, you will be surprised at the distance you can cover. Also, the descent is quite steep, and weak-kneed (in the literal sense) walkers will wail and wobble discontentedly as they descend. Although I see all sorts of improbable foot gear—sandals, sneakers, etc. (I even read that stiletto heals have been found on the trail), definitely wear good hiking boots on this walk.

Toilet Facilities: At the parking lot and near the base of the summit

Refreshments: A small bar near the parking lot

Getting There: From Westport, continue west for about six miles (9.6 kilometers) on R335 to the parking lot at the trail head. Two or three daily buses roll by here from Westport.

Trail Notes

___ 1. From the parking lot, just follow the rocky trail straight up. Other people will probably be on the trail, and you will see a large statue of the Virgin Mary along the way.
___ 2. After about an hour (you have turned right and are walking along the other side of the mountain), you will reach the base of the final climb. As you will clearly note, this is a good point to begin your return. Although the final ascent is quite arduous, the return trip down can be dangerous. However, many people have made it to the summit without mishap. Should you choose to make the final ascent, do so with great caution.

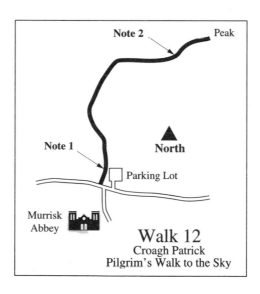

Walk 12
Croagh Patrick
Pilgrim's Walk to the Sky

Suggestions for More Walking

The O.S. map indicated the possibility of continuing on to Louisburg or Westport. However, I saw nothing to indicate this possibility. On the other hand, you can always turn around when you have had enough. Also, see Walk 11 for another possibility.

Walk 13: Cliffs of Moher

Walk: Cliff Walk

Optional time
& distance

General Description

Although remote, the Cliffs of Moher offer some of the best cliff scenery anywhere in the world. The cliffs are defined by a sheer granite wall that drops precipitously for 700 feet at a 180 degree angle into an invariably angry sea. Swirling eddies rise and swell at cliff's bottom as waves pound the striated cliffs. Inclement weather produces a wind-swept, almost terrifying night full of rain even at midday.

Even a short trek along the path will result in many indelible impressions of one towering precipice after another. Seabirds cruise carefree hundreds of feet below, but the sounds of crashing waves will terrify even the least timorous walker. Even if you do not venture far from the tourist center, the nearby 1853 O'Briens Tower allows for some of the best views anywhere along the cliffs.

Optional Maps: O.S. Discovery Series Map #51

Time/Distance: Optional: you can go as far as you wish or as far as you feel comfortable. Regardless of how far you go, the views will be superb and well worth the drive to this remote spot.

Difficulties: A number of climbs in both directions; also, extreme caution should be taken as you walk along the path especially during rainy and/or windy weather.

Toilet Facilities: At the tourist center; some privacy farther out

Refreshments: At the tourist center

Getting There: This walk can be completed from Galway, which is about a ninety-minute vehicular cruise to the cliffs. Alternately, there are a lot of rooms available at Lisdoonvarna about nine miles (14.4 kilometers) from the cliffs.

Trail Notes

___ 1. Take the path from the visitor's center which goes to your left before you enter the center's door and continue to the cliff's edge.
___ 2. From cliff's edge you can go left or right. When I was at the cliffs, the path to the left was temporarily closed; however, hikers were walking along the trail with impunity (stay behind the fence as much as possible). To the right, you are safest walking behind the fence; however, you must go up to the trail at regular intervals in order to avoid barbed-wired fields. On a windy day this can seem perilous.

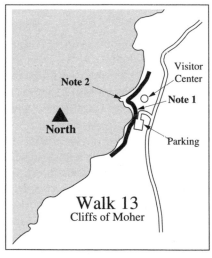

Walk 13
Cliffs of Moher

Suggestions for More Walking

The Burren Way intersects with the cliff path south of Doolin and allows the possibility of a circular route beginning and ending in Doolin. South of the visitor center, the Burren Way coincides with the cliff walk. Due lack of public transport there is no possibility of a one-way trek along this path.

Walk 14: Aran Islands (Galway)

Walk: Inishmore Island from Dun Aonghasa to Kilronan

130 minutes
6.5 miles (10.5 km)

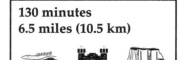

General Description

Located about fifteen nautical miles from Galway, Inishmore, Inishmaan, and Inisheer Islands (collectively known as the Aran Islands) rise rockily from Galway Bay. Today, you will take a ferry out to Inishmore, largest of the three islands, and enjoy excellent views of these three emerald isles as you approach by sea. The islands have been inhabited for millennia and you may survey several prehistoric as well as medieval sites.

Disembarking at Inishmore Island, you will stand solemnly on the terra firma that may be the stone-fence capital of the universe. On this tiny two-by-nine-mile (3.2 by 14.4 kilometers) island, there are several thousand miles of artfully arranged stones that (as a result of centuries of tedious, laborious toil) function as fences. After duly noting the solemnity of your arrival here, you will take a mini bus up to Dun Aonghasa, a venerable vestige of ancient Ireland and one of Europe's finest prehistoric sites. Poised impregnably at the edge of two-hundred-foot cliffs with landward sides protected by three heavily fortified lines of defense, Dun Aonghasa inspired awe and terror in the breasts of potential invaders.

The trek uphill to Dun Aonghasa is a visual delight as you wind your way along a stonily demarcated lane and savor the antiquity of an almost unique monument of prehistory. Were the stones yellow, you would believe Oz loomed ahead. Sitting astride the ocean, Dun Aonghasa needs no walls on its ocean side—the cliffs are unscalable and the vistas are superlative. Given the numberless stones on Inishmore Island, hundreds of such fortresses could have been constructed, but there is only one Dun Aonghasa.

After surveying this lofty monument, you will descend along the same path and begin the trek back to Kilronan across this island of barren aspect where I saw not more than a few solitary trees. As Dun Aonghasa begins to disappear, you will skirt a lovely sandy beach where bold walkers can master cold waters on warm summer days. If you are intrigued by the swimming aspect of this walk, there are a couple of other, rockier beaches along the way to Kilronan. Continuing along the trail, you will gaze continuously out to sea where fishing boats plod slowly in the choppy waters. In the distance, the mainland's rolling coast rises mystically in the haze even on a sunny day. At trail's edge, you will encounter hundreds of varieties of wild flowers and dodge the numerous butterflies that flit aimlessly about. You will also pass a variety of ruins, including the crumbling remains of several medieval stone churches. Near trek's end you will traverse the banks of a fresh-water lake that is home to a congenial family of freely floating, long-necked swans. Back in Kilronan, there is not much to do beyond power shopping for the renowned Aran sweaters that are named for these lovely islands.

The Aran Islands have been linked with Galway because I was not able to unearth a suitable walk into Galway. However, fascinating Galway with its vigorous pub life is Western Ireland's first city and a good base for exploring the Aran Islands. Students enliven the atmosphere and strolling about town visiting the dozens (perhaps hundreds) of pubs seems to be *de rigueur* most evenings. Galway, like most of Ireland's cities, is quintessential gaelic ambiance but not encumbered by many not-to-be-missed historic monuments. However, during daylight hours, you may wish to visit sixteenth-century Lynch's Castle which is home to some menacing gray gargoyles, the Roman Catholic Cathedral which was designed in 1957 as a massive, black marble domed structure that raised the ire of local reactionaries, the fourteenth-century, also gargoyled Church of St. Nicholas where Columbus reportedly prayed on the way to what was to him The New World, and the Nora Barnacle House where James Joyce stayed and was supposedly inspired by the eponymous Nora.

Optional Maps: O.S. map The Aran Islands or the O.S. Discovery Series Map #51; also other locally available guides/maps

Time/Distance: 2 hours 10 minutes/6.5 miles (10.5 kilometers)

Difficulties: A short climb to Dun Aonghasa

Toilet Facilities: At restaurants and pubs near Dun Aonghasa and at Kilronan; some privacy

Refreshments: At restaurants and pubs near Dun Aonghasa and at Kilronan

Getting There: Ferries leave from Galway or Rossaveel, about 24 miles (38.5 kilometers) from Galway (also from Doolin near the Cliffs of Moher). The Tourist Office at Galway has information and schedules for all services. If you go to Rossaveel, please note that language terrorists have painted over or removed English language signs in this area necessitating vigilance in coming and going by car to Rossaveel. Once on the island, simply jump on one of the mini buses. Make it clear that you only wish to go to Dun Aonghasa, unless you wish to take an island tour before embarking on foot (which is a good idea if you have enough time). The more leisurely or earth-friendly walker will hire a fast-galloping, horse-drawn wagon as transport.

Trail Notes

_____ 1. The driver will drop you at an intersection beyond which no vehicles may enter. He will point you in the right direction (you can see you destination from where you stand). From Dun Aonghasa, simply retrace your steps back to where the bus dropped you.
_____ 2. Returning to the point where the bus dropped you, go right at the intersection along the road from where the bus arrived.
_____ 3. Take the path that goes behind the sandy beach.
_____ 4. When you reach a narrow, asphalt road, go left in the direction of the coast.

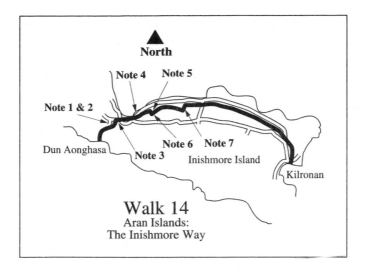

North

Note 4   Note 5

Note 1 & 2

Dun Aonghasa

Note 6   Note 7

Note 3   Inishmore Island

Kilronan

Walk 14
Aran Islands:
The Inishmore Way

___ 5. Turn right on the second grassy path, just before you reach the coast. (You can also continue to follow the road which you will eventually rejoin again.)

___ 6. Walking along that grassy path, take the first path to the left.

___ 7. When you reach a dead end, go left and down until you rejoin the road and go right all the way into Kilronan.

Suggestions for More Walking

There are no official trails in or around Galway. However, you can take the bus to the far end of Salthill and walk back along the coast to the town center of Galway. From Barna, the next town on the coast, you may be able to walk back along the coast alternating with some road walking. There are numerous opportunities for walking on Inishmore Island and also the other Aran Islands. Consult the tourist office, locally produced guides, and the maps mentioned above.

Walk 15: Limerick

Walk: O'Brien's Bridge to Limerick

180 minutes
9 miles (14.4 km)

General Description

O'Brien's Bridge is the name of a town and a bridge, and although today's walk begins at the bridge, you can stroll into the cute but ordinary town of O'Brien's Bridge where there is not much to do beyond examining the local commerce or lounging in a pub. However, since the trek to Limerick is so alluring, you will probably want to embark immediately without detour from the bridge.

After a quick jaunt from Limerick by bus or taxi to O'Brien's Bridge, you will survey the trail ahead and quickly descend to the canal. Immediately, you will observe a sign admonishing that it is unsafe to bathe along the canal.

Paradoxically, above this sign rests a round life preserver of substantial diameter. Properly counseled against illicit swimming, you will stride dryly along the towpath, a broad swath of grass-covered, elevated earth paralleling the canal. Although the road is not distant from the canal at this point, you will feel far and away from urban woes, since the road is concealed by a dense strip of trees. On the opposite side of the canal, strands of tall trees stretch to the tops of the mist-covered hills that dominate the horizon. An occasional church spire, neatly framed by the embracing forest, rises in the distance.

Continuing along the trail, you will experience the sights, sounds, and smells of rural Ireland and dodge the gangs of marauding sheep awaiting at strategic intervals to "baa" the unwary walker. Glancing into the canal you will note an agglomeration of superb water lillies that Monet would have been anxious to paint. Farther along, you will encounter towering gold haystacks, ample fodder for many a cool winter day. Van Gogh would have climbed over fields of French haystacks to get his brush on these superb Irish stacks, which were being heaped high by corpulent, brazenly bare-chested farmers in the traditional manner with a pitchfork when I passed by.

Approaching Limerick, you will cross the wide waters of the River Shannon and be confronted by the crumbling ruins of a castle keep. Standing for centuries in solemn vigilance, this medieval monument still awaits some unknown foe. At this point you will follow the Shannon River Walk, a lovely path used by many Limerickers for recreational purposes. Weary walkers will appreciate the benches which are strategically placed to ensure a leisurely afternoon on the trail. Here and there fishermen doze quietly while waiting for fish to jump into their nets. Closer to Limerick, King John's Castle comes into view, marking the beginning of the transition from rural to urban.

This is truly a through-the-back-door walk as you enter a major city along an almost forgotten nineteenth-century canal towpath which eventually leads you along a brick road and past an abandoned factory—a derelict relic of the Industrial Revolution. The final entry into the heart of Limerick is initially rather disturbing as you hear the jarring sounds of city traffic for the first time in a couple hours. You will soon feel at home as the first visible commercial sign proudly announces "Texaco/Dunkin' Donuts."

Limerick, with only about 80,000 inhabitants, is sparsely populated Ireland's fourth largest city. Limerick's history begins early in the ninth century when Viking marauders established a base here for pillaging the surrounding countryside. These horned-helmeted vandals were eventually driven out, only to be replaced by Norman invaders in the late twelfth century. Several centuries later, the Normans themselves were expelled and replaced in the mid-seventeenth century by English imperialists en route to world domination. The English remained until the War of Independence that ended in the early 1920s.

Limerick's turbulent past is evidenced by its major tourist attraction, King John's Castle. This venerable thirteenth-century fortress still rises valiantly along the banks of the Shannon River. Inside, you may tour the walls and enjoy the recently completed exhibits on Viking history. Not far from King John's Castle is the late twelfth-century St. Mary's Cathedral (Limerick's oldest building). Inside you will want to survey the misericords (side chairs) which are the only surviving examples in Ireland and depict, via a series of intricate carvings, a titanic struggle between good and evil. Return in the evening for a sound and light show about Limerick's past. If you crave more adventures in the history of Limerick, you will want to visit the aptly named

Limerick Museum which houses a fascinating collection of photographs dating back to the mid-nineteenth century. Cathedral enthusiasts will stroll over to St. John's Cathedral, which was constructed in the neo-Gothic style; this nineteenth-century cathedral boasts the tallest spire in Ireland.

Optional Maps: Currently, no Discovery Series maps have been completed for this area. There is a Lough Derg Way brochure with a not-very-detailed map available at the tourist office, or the old O. S. ½ inch to 1 mile maps #17 and #18 that may be helpful. However, the trail is fairly well marked and you should have no problems.

Time/Distance: 3 hours/9 miles (14.4 kilometers)

Difficulties: None

Toilet Facilities: At the pub about two hours into the walk and in Limerick; some privacy

Refreshments: At the pub about two hours into the walk and in Limerick

Getting There: During the summer, two buses per day run from Limerick to O'Brien's Bridge; during the rest of the year, there are only several per week. However, long lines of taxis await you in front of the Limerick tourist office.

Trail Notes

___ 1. The bus or cab will drop you at O'Brien's Bridge (the town O'Brien's Bridge is on the other side of the bridge). Cross the bridge, and go to your right and down to the banks of the canal on the far side of the bridge from the road.

___ 2. About 20 minutes after you pass the bridge to Cloonlara (the only bridge since O'Brien's Bridge), you will go left and away from the towpath where you will see an arrow. Continue to the gate that leads to an asphalt road. From this point the trail is well marked and winds along country lanes for about thirty-five to forty minutes.

___ 3. When you make a sharp left onto an asphalt road with an

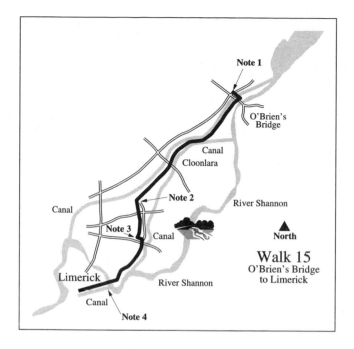

obscure graystone pub on the corner (a good place to stop for a mid-walk beverage), continue along the road for a couple minutes, and then turn right along a canal towpath. There is a pole here but the sign had been removed when I came by.

___ 4. From the River Shannon you will enter Limerick along the towpath of a narrow canal. The first street you walk along is Lock Quay which you follow until the first brown "i" (for information) sign becomes visible where you turn left. Turn right where you see the Burger King and Penney's; you will soon be at the tourist office.

Suggestions for More Walking

You could lengthen this walk by taking the bus up to Killaloe or even further by taking a taxi up the east bank of Lough Derg. You could shorten the walk by about an hour by starting at the Cloonlara Bridge. At the Killaloe tourist office, you can pick up the "Walks in the Killaloe District" brochure that describes three circular walks from 4.5 to 15 miles (7.2 to 24 kilometers).

Walk 16: Tralee

Walk: Spa to Tralee

General Description

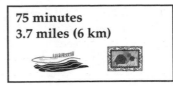

75 minutes
3.7 miles (6 km)

Your starting point, the semi-aban-
doned village of Spa, will not hold you long unless you have decided
to have lunch at the Oyster Bar which specializes in a variety of savory
(in their own estimation) seafood meals; otherwise, there is nothing to
detain you from a quick walk down to the beach where you will begin
to trace the sheltered coast of the Tralee Bay. Although the waves lap
quietly along the shoreline, the erosive effects of time have had their
effect—rocks are piled high everywhere in defense of the battered
coast. Continuing along the coast, you will enjoy excellent views
of the hills and towns on the opposite side of the bay; and Tralee,
which is remotely visible in the distance, becomes less remote with
each step. This is a magnificent short walk with excellent views of
the entire inlet throughout—hills drop gently to the coast, a patchwork of earth-tone farms decorates the slope, clouds swirl in misty
chaos, fishing vessels bounce lazily over the calm waters, and graceful swans lurk at a comely fresh-water pond. Not too far from the
trail (look for the windmill) is diminutive Blennerville where there
are a couple of distracting attractions. The circa 1800 windmill that
guided you here has been completely restored and functions as it
did almost 200 years ago. A display on the ground floor of this
five-story behemoth tells you everything you wanted to know and
more about mills and milling. Next door you can view the Emigra-
tion Exhibition which portrays hardships endured by Irish
emigrants to America in the nineteenth century. Blennerville is also
the terminus for the narrow-gauge, nineteenth-century Tralee Light
Railway which steams (literally) the short mile and a half (2.5 kilometers) between Blennerville and Tralee. You can elect at this point
to ride in one of the original carriages back to Tralee or you can
walk and take the fun round trip.

The final approach to Tralee follows a relic of the Industrial Revolution, a canal towpath with some of the original hardware still visible. The canal is a remnant of a kinder, gentler time when transportation was casual and didn't move at a break-neck pace. You will enjoy this time trek, and future walkers may enjoy an embellished experience since plans are being made to clean up the canal and revive the towpath as a recreational haven.

Tralee is a very busy town with a family-oriented agenda. Kerry the Kingdom is the top attraction and one of the largest museums in Ireland. The museum exhibits serve as a historical narrative for County Kerry. Outstanding among the exhibits is the lower-level reconstruction of medieval Tralee that you will traverse in a small cart at a medieval snail's pace while listening to an explanatory monologue. Strolling to or from Kerry the Kingdom, you will want to tour the Town Park (one of Ireland's largest) which is home to a sumptuous collection of the finest roses in the universe; if you are here in August you may even participate in the Rose of Tralee Festival and lend support for your favorite Irish beauty who will represent the town and festival as queen. At the Aquadome, Tralee's newest attraction, adults may relax in a whirlpool/sauna/steamroom paradise while children bounce about a wave pool, ride rapid rapids, and tumble headlong down a giant waterslide.

Optional Maps: O.S. Discovery Series Map #71

Time/Distance: 1 hour 15 minutes / 3.7 miles (6 kilometers)

Difficulties: None

Toilet Facilities: At Tralee, Spa or a short detour to Blennerville; some privacy

Refreshments: At Tralee, Spa, or a short detour to Blennerville

Getting There: Buses run occasionally to Spa on their way to Fenit; however, it is much more convenient and not too expensive to take a taxi to Spa. Get off at the center of this wide-spot-in-the-road where there is an abandoned supermarket, a decaying telephone booth and a very large seafood restaurant called the Oyster Bar.

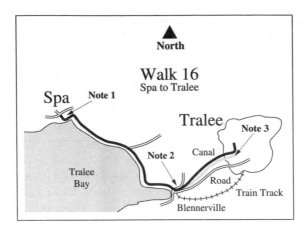

Trail Notes

___ 1. Follow the narrow road down to the beach and turn left in the direction of Tralee. You can walk on the beach or along the stone barrier behind the beach.

___ 2. Just before the windmill, you will begin to follow the canal. Fatigued footsters can use the hourly (in the summer) steam train from Blennerville to arrive at Tralee.

___ 3. When you are forced from the canal, walk to the traffic circle and turn left. You are in town.

Suggestions for More Walking

To shorten this walk you may take the steam train, which runs hourly during the summer, back from Blennerville. Originally, I was going to include a ten-mile (16 kilometer) walk into Tralee from a point just east of Camp where the trail intersects N86. This is a portion of the Dingle Way and is clearly visible in the O.S. map mentioned above. This looks like an interesting walk; but, there is no way of explaining this place to a bus driver (although a signpost is visible to the eagle eyed). However, if you check out the area first by car and then have a taxi drive you out, I suspect you will be well rewarded. The next two walks (17 and 18) can also be completed from Tralee.

Walk 17: Dingle Peninsula

Walk: Slea Head to Ventry Beach

| 120 minutes |
| 5.2 miles (8.3 km) |

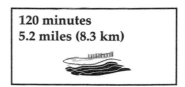

General Description

Nature experience par excellence, this trek between wild Slea Head and mild Ventry Beach offers some of Ireland's finest scenic miles. Stunning views of the frighteningly ferocious Atlantic Ocean and Ireland's most westerly Blasket Islands await at Slea Head where you begin to follow the trail back to Ventry. After several minutes or hours of gazing into the vast tableau of the bounding main crashing upon craggy coast and windswept islands, avert your gaze from the ocean to the towering hills haphazardly partitioned by jagged stone fences that drop precipitously to the coast. Hollywood could find no more magnificent image for the essence of Ireland, and segments of the Tom Cruise/ Nicole Kidman film *Far and Away* were filmed around Slea Head. For a snack and comfortable oceanside vantage point, perch yourself in the Enchanted Forest Cafe where better-than-Hollywood views extend for ever.

Tear yourself from Slea Head's grandeur and begin to ascend along a rocky pathway that snakes its way ever higher while offering increasingly impressive views of Slea Head and the foreboding gray waves of the Atlantic Ocean. As Slea Head disappears, you will pace a path high above the ocean and the busy road that skirts the coast. Tread nimbly high above the mechanized mania with only the occasional sheep as a companion. You are truly off the beaten path.

To your right here and there, you will notice prehistoric stone structures in the shape of beehives. It is believed that the 400 or so still in existence and currently used for storage or nothing at all were the humble abodes of early Christian monks who sought to be alone—but given the proximity of the huts, not completely alone. Beyond the huts, the ocean continues to dominate the horizon as fishing boats skim precariously over the ceaseless waves. Although you can see for endless miles, avert your glance occasionally to enjoy the wild flowers that bloom brilliantly at your feet and the lovely maze of crumbling stone walls that intricately lace the verdant slopes.

Near walk's end, you will be rewarded by expansive perspectives of lengthy Ventry Beach and stride past the long-abandoned stone houses that dot the landscape. Sandy Ventry beach serves as today's trek's terminus. On a clear day you may wish to half bake (full baking on an Irish beach is virtually impossible) on the beach and challenge the hearty Atlantic waves. When clouds dominate, Ventry Beach is virtually abandoned, and a solo trek across the mist enshrouded beach is a fitting end to a wild Irish experience.

Optional Maps: O.S. Discovery Series Map #70

Time/Distance: 2 hours / 5.2 miles (8.3 kilometers)

Difficulties: A difficult climb out of Slea Head

Toilet Facilities: At the cafe near Slea Head; some privacy

Refreshments: There is a small store across from the church where you can purchase refreshments. There is also a cafe where you will descend from the bus.

Getting There: Take the bus from Ventry church about a mile (1.6 kilometers) west of the small town of Ventry (which is about five miles/8 kilometers west from Dingle) in the direction of Slea Head. Buses pass by here twice daily during the summer, and the schedule is available at the Dingle tourist office or the Tralee bus station (066)23566. You cannot get off at Slea Head (there is a large white statue of the Virgin Mary at the site), so ask the driver to let you off at the first parking lot around the corner which is called Dun Chaoin. Just ahead on the road, you will see a large red building with bears and trees painted on the facade called the "Enchanted Forest Magical World of Holidays and Seasons for the Young at Heart" (How do workers efficiently identify this long-named place when answering the phone?). There is a cafe inside; old-hearted walkers are not invited.

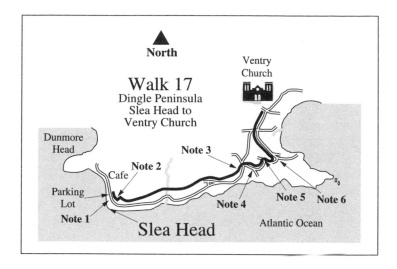

Trail Notes

___ 1. Walk back along the road in the direction of Ventry. In about two to three minutes you will leave the road to the left where you will see a post with a yellow arrow. Pull the metal gate open (be sure to shut it), and walk upwards along the fence.

___ 2. You will reach a point where you have to make a sharp left turn along a wire fence (if you could walk straight ahead through the fence you would be going in the correct direction). In a couple seconds you will see some faded yellow markers which lead you over a portion of the fence where the barbed wire has been removed. You must go over the fence and to your right and then back down to the fence that parallels the road and continue in the direction of Ventry. From this point you will be following fences and stone walls—the trail is well marked but be vigilant.

___ 3. When you reach an asphalt road (R559), you will go left and then take a quick right. Both turns are marked.

___ 4. Continue left when you reach a fork.

___ 5. When the road takes a sharp left, go right on a path.

___ 6. When you reach a dead end at an asphalt road go left and continue on to Ventry Church. (You will see one arrow leading you along this road and another arrow leading right to the beach. If you elect to follow the beach, which is more picturesque, you will have to wade across a shallow stream.)

Suggestions for More Walking

You could extend this walk about one mile (1.6 kilometers) by taking the bus to Dunquin, or you could follow the trail back to town of Ventry or even Dingle (an extra 3.5 miles/5.6 kilometers). For a shorter walk, you could leave your car at the intersection mentioned in Note 3. Ferries from Dunquin dock at remote Great Blasket Island where you can enjoy a variety of unmarked trails which appear on the map listed above. Also, consider Walks 16 and 1.

Walk 18: Dingle

Walk: Lispole to Dingle

General Description

150 minutes
6.7 miles (10.7 km)

Incredibly shrinking Lispole is almost completely enshrouded by encroaching vegetation. A shop and a post office comprise the commercial sector, which is flanked by a few cottages and outlying homes. Cuteness abounds, but you will want to quickly survey the scene and traverse the tiny Poteen Bridge where the trail begins. On the initial trek from Lispole, you will climb through a verdant passageway lined by bountifully blooming shrubbery while glancing back over your shoulder to scenes of the valley below. Surveying the heights, you will imbibe stunning views of intensely green An Cnoc peak which rises paternally above the trail. Beneath the shadow of mighty An Cnoc, you will enjoy award-winning vistas of green hills, an inviting valley, and the expansive ocean. The trail seems to have an alpine aspect about it and imparts a feeling of great loneliness even though you are

never far from civilization. This is quintessential, quaint Ireland as depicted in the tourist brochures.

Soon you will pass the temptingly nomered "Mountain Road Whole Food B&B" which is romantically situated far from the madding crowd. Also, watch for the nearby hyper-intensely white-washed house that stands in surrealistic defiance of encroaching verdancy. A special surprise awaits as you traverse Lisdargan, a tiny hamlet remotely tucked away from twentieth-century perils with its own B&B. Approaching Dingle, you will cross a tiny plank bridge over a bubbling brook, and survey the stone houses in varying states of decay that litter the trail in a romantic tableau of times long forgotten. The final descent is along a pleasant country lane with great views of the Dingle Town, Dingle Bay, and distant hills.

Superbly situated, visually stunning Dingle, which slopes gracefully downhill into a lovely bay, rightly deserves its growing popularity. A lively, lovely place with a stream running through it, nautical Dingle sports a picturesque port where mighty masts create an artificial seagoing forest.

Atmosphere is everything here, and those who savor pub life will prolong their sojourn ad infinitum in order to tour the several dozen pubs that serve less than two thousand local inhabitants (a small town but still the largest population center on the Dingle Peninsula). If time permits, you may wish to stagger into St. Mary's Church which was built in the nineteenth century, but there is not much to see. You may also wish to watch for the dolphin named Fungi who lurks about Dingle Bay and attracts hordes of boaters and wet-suited swimmers. Fishermen may wish to take one of the fishing excursions from the pier. Although there is not much to do, this is a truly wonderful place. I was in no hurry to leave.

Optional Maps: O.S. Discovery Series Map #70

Time/Distance: 2 hours 30 minutes / 6.7 miles (10.7 kilometers)

Difficulties: Several short climbs

Toilet Facilities: Only at Dingle; some privacy

Refreshments: Store at Lispole; stores, restaurants, pubs at Dingle

Getting There: Bus Eireann departs Dingle from in front of the Super Valu grocery store near the harbor. Ask the bus driver to drop you off at the post office in Lispole. Information about departure times is available at the tourist office or the Tralee bus station (066)23566.

Trail Notes

___ 1. Walk back over a bridge in the direction of Dingle, and turn right along a narrow asphalt road. You will see a direction post pointing you in this direction.
___ 2. Turn left at the first four-way intersection which is waymarked.
___ 3. About thirty minutes into the walk you will turn right away from the asphalt road where you see a waymark, and then turn left in a few minutes where you will also see a waymark.
___ 4. After crossing a river you will turn left on a gravel road and descend into Dingle.

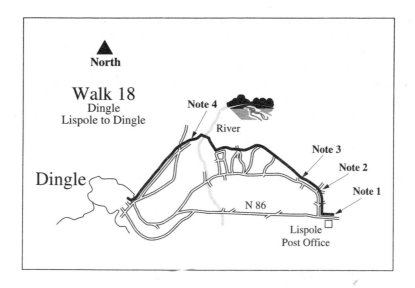

▲
North

Walk 18
Dingle
Lispole to Dingle

Note 4

River

Note 3

Note 2

Note 1

Dingle

N 86

Lispole
Post Office

Suggestions for More Walking

There is no possibility of shortening this walk; however, you could lengthen it by about 5.5 miles (8.8 kilometers) by taking the bus down to Anascaul; you could also extend this walk by a variety of other lengths since the bus to Tralee intersects the trail at several points. Also consider Walks 16 and 17.

Walk 19: Killarney National Park

Walk: Galway's Bridge to Killarney (Muckross Abbey) via the Kerry Way

170 minutes
7.5 miles (12 km)

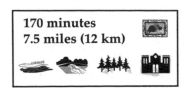

General Description

Galway's Bridge, located at the periphery of a full blooming enchanted valley, is simply a bend in the road where you will descend from the bus and admire the lonely but lovely abandoned church that marks the starting point for today's adventure. After surveying the church, you become immediately detached from the mechanized world of sound and speed. As an added bonus, you will glide along a trail that is easily negotiable throughout, with railroad ties placed over more saturated stretches, helping you enjoy the views rather than watching out for ubiquitous mud.

Only a few minutes into the walk, you will begin to ascend along a deeply forested narrow path and be greeted by abounding views of distant, serrated peaks jutting forth into swirling rain clouds as the path becomes level. Closer to the path, moss-covered boulders threaten to roll down slippery slopes onto the valley floor, and ubiquitous moss-covered fences resemble a sort of organic protoplasm splattered about the trail. Even by Irish standards verdancy overwhelms, yielding an intensely green experience throughout this magnificent valley. Continuing along, you will notice a slender waterfall tumbling with great alacrity along a chute of jagged rocks creating a winsome sonic ambiance and resulting in a slippery stream that you will follow for a while. Later you will trace the course of tree lined river that creates soothing sounds for your increased tranquility. Approaching the grounds of Muckross House, you will delight in excellent views of two lovely bodies of water, Lakes Muckross and Leane. Both have an ultra-pristine appearance—rocky beaches and clear, cool water encircled by pine-covered hills sloping sleekly into the tranquil waters. Beyond the lakes, Killarney National Park's Muckross House rises in formal magnificence from the surrounding miles of moss-covered nature. Constructed in the Elizabethan style during the 1840's Muckross House is a superb mansion that is well worthy of the time for a short tour. Watch for the well-aged bottles in the wine cellar. Surrounding the house are extensive formal gardens that you will traverse in order to visit the stunning remains of fifteenth-century Muckross Abbey and its surrounding cemetery. Founded by Franciscan friars in the this remote part of Ireland, much of Muckross Abbey is still intact, particularly the church and cloisters.

Killarney is basically a tourist town, but a very nice one—not too garish with an astonishing number of rooms for rent at all spending levels, plenty of restaurants, some not-too-tacky souvenirs, and a great location for exploring the surrounding countryside. However, you will not be in seclusion; watch for sharp elbows belonging to the throngs of bus tourists who are drawn to Killarney, the horse-drawn-carriage capital of Ireland and perhaps the entire world. These primitive conveyances are here, there and everywhere looking for you, the well-heeled tourist.

Killarney's major (perhaps just largest) tourist site is Anglican St. Mary's Cathedral which was constructed in the late nineteenth century and merits a quick look around. Automobile buffs will want to reserve some time for the National Museum of Irish Transport. The fascinating exhibit includes a number of unusual vehicles including a rare 1955 Mercedes 300SL gullwing model and a one-of-a-kind 1907 Silver Stream. In addition to the cars, there is also a collection of automotive memorabilia including a variety of rare posters.

As usual it is the atmosphere not the historical sights that captivate in Irish towns and cities, so spend as much time as possible out and about in this area of great natural beauty. Killarney National Park, which extends around Lough Leane up to the city of Killarney, is one of Ireland's finest centers of natural beauty. Much of today's walk transpires within park boundaries, but for walkers with extra time there are plenty of opportunities to trek through the forest. A park map is available at the information center behind Muckross House. In particular, fifteenth-century Ross Castle and Ross Island are not far and warrant a quick trek.

Optional Maps: O.S. Discovery Series Map #78

Time/Distance: 2 hours 50 minutes/7.5 miles (12 kilometers)

Difficulties: About 20 minutes of tolerable climbing soon after departure from Galway's Bridge, afterwards a number of minor ups and downs

Toilet Facilities: At Killarney and at Muckross House; some privacy

Refreshments: Restaurants, pubs, and stores at Killarney and refreshments at Muckross House

Getting There: If you have a car, it is best to leave it at the parking lot to your left, about two miles (3 kilometers) from Killarney's center. This is easy to find because it is where the carriage drivers congregate. This parking lot is across from the gate where you will emerge from the park. By doing this you will eliminate two miles (3 kilometers) of road walking. Wave at the bus, and the driver will stop. The alternative is to take a carriage back to town from the parking lot at walk's end. Buses from Killarney to Kenmare via Moll's Gap (you must take the bus that goes via Moll's Gap) run two to three times daily. The bus driver will know the location of Galway's Bridge, but you may have to jog his memory by describing it as being "where the road turns sharply right and there is an abandoned church." Watch for the church as the bus turns right (it is the only church on the way). Schedules are available at the Killarney bus station (tel. 34777).

Trail Notes

___ 1. Stand in front of the church looking down the road from where the bus has arrived. Walk to your right along a narrow asphalt road (ignore the sign post across the road to your left). You will see a sign post.

___ 2. About eight minutes into the walk, you will turn left where you will see a sign post. (If you follow the sign leading straight ahead, you will end up in Kenmare.)

___ 3. Approaching the road (N71) you will come to a fork where you will go left, keeping the river to your right.

___ 4. When you reach the road (N71) go directly across through the trees on the other side of the road and to the narrow asphalt road where you turn left and follow this narrow road as it turns right a couple minutes later over a small bridge. You will have to climb over a small gate as you continue along this road past

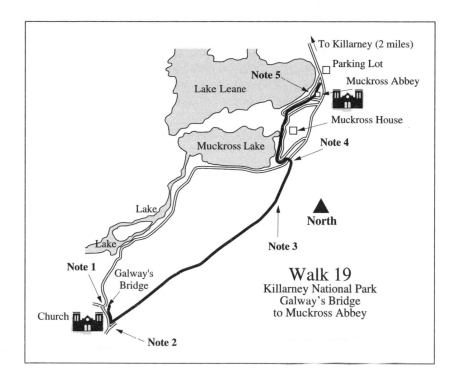

To Killarney (2 miles)

Parking Lot

Note 5

Lake Leane

Muckross Abbey

Muckross House

Muckross Lake

Note 4

Lake

▲ North

Lake

Note 3

Note 1

Galway's Bridge

Walk 19
Killarney National Park
Galway's Bridge
to Muckross Abbey

Church

Note 2

Muckross House and eventually Muckross Abbey.

___ 5. At Muckross Abbey you will reach a fork where you will go left
(the entrance to the abbey is to the right) and follow the road out
to your car.

Suggestions for More Walking

This walk can be shortened to about two miles (3 kilometers) by taking
the bus to the location mentioned in Note 4, and it can be combined
with Walk 19 for a full day's outing. Also, this is part of the Kerry Way
which ranges widely over the Iveragh Peninsula. The entire route is
covered by O.S. Discovery Series Maps 70, 78, 83, and 84. There is also
a very useful *Kerry Way Map Guide* (1:50,000) published by Cork Kerry
Tourism which is available at many stores in the area or contact the

Tourist House in Cork (021)273251. Also, see Walk 21 for another attractive section of the Kerry Way. The area west of Sneem is quite attractive and is served by public transportation. There are also a number of circular routes that can be devised within the park. Even if you are short of time, a walk around the grounds of Muckross House and Abbey are well worth a few stolen moments. Once on the grounds of Muckross House, it is usually possible to find a carriage to drive you around the grounds and deliver you to your car or back to town.

Walk 20: Glenbeigh

Walk: A Walk High on the Kerry Way

120 minutes
5 miles (8 km)

General Description

Glenbeigh is tourist friendly but not tourist overrun, and a good day excursion for those sojourning in Killarney—the pace slackens from slow to slower. If you wish to spend the night however, there are numerous B&Bs and also the historic Glenbeigh Hotel which is noted for fine food, odd but comfortable rooms, and excellent service. Most Glenbeigh sojourners are here for the truly superb beach which wraps several miles around a peninsula jutting boldly into Dingle Bay. Massive dunes are ringed by great expanses of fine sand and the intense green hills in the distance stand in marked contrast to the sable colored sand. This is one of Ireland's premier beaches which, as a result of the Irish climate, is relatively abandoned—even on a nice day.

As the trek begins, you will climb in a wide arc from the coast, and be rewarded by outstanding views of the beach, Dingle Bay, and a towering command of the entire area from your peak-top perch. Reaching the heights and turning back in the direction of Glenbeigh, you will begin a long, lonely plateau ramble that affords outstanding views of hill and dale. The views from hilltop are realllllllly BIG—you can see almost to New Jersey. The rocky terrain continues to roll, while distant views continue to beckon vista-weary eyes. As you clamber over the final ridge, be prepared for knockout views of Glenbeigh deep in the valley below. The steep but picturesque descent continues to be a visual delight as you wind your way in and out of forested areas while seldom losing sight of vast land and seascapes. If you have the time for this pleasant detour well off the beaten tourist track, you will not be disappointed.

Optional Maps: O.S. Discovery Series Map #78

Time/Distance: 2 hours / 5 miles (8 kilometers)

Difficulties: A difficult twenty-minute climb from the beach and some minor ups and downs.

Toilet Facilities: At Glenbeigh and near White Strand Beach

Refreshments: At Glenbeigh and near White Strand Beach

Getting There: This walk starts at the Glenbeigh town center which is about twenty miles (32 kilometers) northwest of Killarney and is reachable by the Ring of Kerry bus.

Trail Notes

___ 1. From Glenbeigh's town center walk along the main street directly west.

___ 2. Arriving at a fork a few minutes later, you will go right along the asphalt road (you will see a sign indicating "Ross Beigh Strand" and also a sign indicating "Kerry Way").

___ 3. Ignore the Kerry Way sign going up and to your left; this is where you will return to Glenbeigh. Continue along the road to the beach, which is about 30 minutes from the town center.

___ 4. From the beach, continue along the narrow road that rises as it skirts the coast.

___ 5. When you reach a fork, go left and continue to climb as it winds away from beach.

___ 6. Turn sharply left when you see a "Kerry Way" sign and continue to follow the hilltop path until it descends to a parking lot where you turn right along the road in order to return to Glenbeigh.

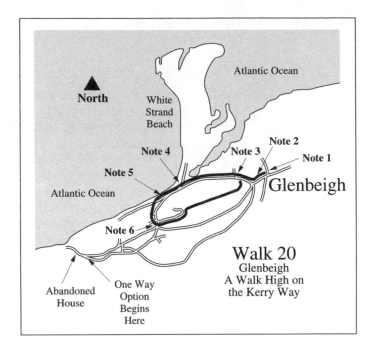

Suggestions for More Walking

This walk can also be completed as a one-way journey by taking a bus or taxi up to where N70 intersects with a minor road, just before you reach an abandoned stone house. However, this is not easy to describe to a bus driver, so it is necessary to scout this site by car or take a taxi. If you decide on this one-way option, walk up the minor road that intersects with N70 and you will begin to see Kerry Way sign posts. This is part of the Kerry Way, which ranges widely over the Iveragh Peninsula. The entire route is covered by O.S. Discovery Series Maps 70, 78, 83, and 84. There is also a very useful *Kerry Way Map Guide* (1:50,000) published by Cork Kerry Tourism which is available at many stores in the area or contact the Tourist House in Cork (021)273251. Also, see Walks 20 and 21 for other attractive sections of the Kerry Way. The area west of Sneem is quite attractive and served by public transportation. You can extend this walk by about four miles (6.4 kilometers) with a loop around the beach.

Walk 21: Kenmare

Walk: Galway's Bridge to Kenmare via the Kerry Way

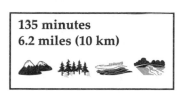

135 minutes
6.2 miles (10 km)

General Description

Galway's Bridge, located at the periphery of a full blooming enchanted valley, is simply a bend in the road where you will descend from the bus and admire the lonely but lovely abandoned church that marks the starting point for today's adventure. Scurrying from the road onto the trail, other tourists soon become only a memory and an awesome sense of preternatural calm permeates the valley as you begin this trek far from the twentieth century. Beginning to stride upon a narrow band of wilderness trail surrounded by florid flora, you will immediately revel in privileged views available only to the walker. As you climb from the valley, be sure to glance over your shoulder for a view of the diminutive church silhouetted against massive mountains. Look back on a regular basis; some of the best views are behind you.

In the distance, gray stone and green grass vie for supremacy on mountains that recede far into the vast horizon throughout this sublimely beautiful area. A fast flowing stream races alongside and great boulders litter the high country in chaotic but aesthetically pleasing disarray. Here and there the sun filters through low-lying clouds creating a beam-like effect and focusing on the majesty of random features in this enchanted landscape. However, most intriguing are the curious long-abandoned structures that greet with stony silence as you continue to trek high above sea level. Who lived here? Why did they leave? What were their lives like? Many such questions arise. In fact, the only humans I have encountered were four shepherds accompanied by two dogs in search of errant sheep. Loneliness abounds.

After about an hour, you reach an apogee where vistas of Kenmare and environs are astonishing—a vast panorama of forested hills combined with views of a distant town and a solitary, pristine lake which form a sort of multi-miled spectacularism seldom found on any walk anywhere. Beginning the final descent, you will marvel repeatedly at the broad, knock-out views of Kenmare lying recumbent on its comely bay. The aura of triumphant tranquility continues to envelope the fortunate walker all the way into Kenmare.

Kenmare, cozily nestled along the peaceful banks of the Kenmare River is an attractively situated valley town encircled by a protective ring of mountains. It is similar in its outdoorsy/touristy atmosphere to Killarney, but smaller and less heavily trampled. I liked Killarney in spite of its commercial patina, but I found Kenmare to be a more restful center for a summer sojourn. The two main streets, where facades have been attractively reconstructed, harbor a variety of savory dining opportunities and a collection of intriguing emporiums that specialize in local crafts. The major tourist attraction is the prosaically nomered, prehistoric Stone Circle which consists of a central stone surrounded by a dozen or so other stones, not exactly Notre Dame Cathedral but the largest such site in this sector of Ireland. Also worthy of a quick inspection is the Kenmare Heritage Centre located within the confines of the tourist office. The exhibits trace the history of Kenmare and County Kerry with a special emphasis on the exquisite lacemaking techniques (including demonstrations) that were originated by industrious Kenmare Convent nuns in the nineteenth century. Kenmare combined with this not-to-be-missed walk described above offers a nonpareil overnight stop on your island tour.

Optional Maps: O.S. Discovery Series Map #78

Time/Distance: 2 hours 15 minutes/6.2 miles (10 kilometers)

Difficulties: A number of ups and downs, most are moderate; the trail can be muddy, and you will have to cross some very shallow streams on large stones.

Toilet Facilities: Only at Kenmare; some privacy

Refreshments: Only at Kenmare

Getting There: Buses from Kenmare to Killarney via Moll's Gap (you must take the bus that goes via Moll's Gap) run two to three times daily. The bus driver will know the location of Galway's Bridge, but you may have to describe it as being "where the road turns sharply left and there is an abandoned church." The ride takes just over twenty minutes. You will pass Moll's Gap where the Avoca shop and the Ladies' View shop are located before arriving at Galway's Bridge. Watch for the church as the bus turns left (it is the only church on the way). Schedules are available at the Kenmare tourist office (tel. 41223).

Trail Notes

___ 1. Stand in front of the church looking down the road where the bus has continued. Walk to your right along a narrow asphalt road (ignore the sign post across the road to your left). You will see a sign post.

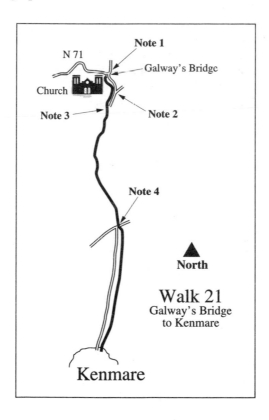

Walk 21
Galway's Bridge
to Kenmare

___ 2. After a few minutes, you will see a sign post leading to your left; DO NOT GO IN THIS DIRECTION, unless you wish to end up in Killarney. Continue straight ahead where there is also a sign post.

___ 3. Do not go right where you see a very florid path which leads to a home. Just continue on the winding trail as it continues upward, ignoring any smaller trails on either side.

___ 4. About midway, you will intersect a narrow asphalt road; continue straight ahead (there is a walker's symbol high on a telephone pole). This road will take you directly into town—just follow the church steeple.

Suggestions for More Walking

Although there is no way of shortening this walk using public transportation, it can be combined with Walk 20 for a full day's outing. Also, this is part of the Kerry Way which ranges widely over the Iveragh Peninsula. The entire route is covered by O.S. Discovery Series Maps 70, 78, 83, and 84. There is also a very useful *Kerry Way Map Guide* (1:50,000) published by Cork Kerry Tourism which is available at many stores in the area or contact the Tourist House in Cork (021)273251. Also, see Walks 20 and 21 for another attractive section of the Kerry Way. The area west of Sneem is quite attractive and served by public transportation.

Walk 22: Dursey Island

Walk: To the End of the Beara Way

180 minutes
8.5 miles (13.6 km)

General Description

No less beautiful, and in some respects more spectacular than the Ring of Kerry, is the Beara Peninsula. Here, the throngs of tourists thin to a trickle, and the peninsula slumbers in tranquil obscurity. You are definitely off the beaten track, and when you reach Dursey Island, there is virtually no tourist track at all.

Passage to Dursey Island is achieved via an antiquated cable car (the only one in all of Ireland) that is controlled by the only man in the world who is more lonely than a Maytag repairman. He normally slumbers in his aging automobile, and you may have to arouse him with gentle tap on the window. I am certain that his retirement or untimely demise is anxiously awaited by legions of lazy and covetous laborers everywhere. As the creaking cable car creeps dutifully along, you will notice the disconcerting Psalm 91 conspicuously framed at eye level with the admonition "Read everyday for protection," and stating "Whoever goes to the Lord for safety/Whoever remains under the protection of the Almighty can say to Him you are my defender and protector...you will keep me safe from all hidden dangers and from all deadly diseases," etc. I assume there is a crashing cable car addendum tacked on somewhere, but I chose to read no further. Only slightly daunted, I averted my gaze from the far-from-calming Psalm to the crashing waves far below and the spectacular views in all directions.

Alighting briskly from the cable car, you will gratefully kiss the secure terra firma and begin to ramble along the coast. Close to the cable-car station, there is an abandoned church and a cemetery where all current residents seem to reside. Although quite barren and almost devoid of trees, Dursey Island has a generally green patina generously interspersed with jagged gray rocks of all descriptions. Beginning the coastal trek, you will enjoy quintessential Irish panoramas on a grand scale—powerful waves crash decisively along the craggy coast; distant mainland coast and barren islands jut prominently into the horizon; low-flying birds cry out unceasingly in stentorian tones; and a few lonely fishermen ply the chronically troubled waters.

Turning inland, you will traverse Kilmichael, Dursey's only hamlet and residence for those who choose not to reside in the cemetery. I saw no one here, making this a not-to-be-missed destination for misanthdropes, not a DROP to be found. And, as far as automobiles are concerned, there are only a few hulks rusting in peace by the cable car dock. Ramble as far as you wish, the views are uniformly superb. Even a short walk reaps the benefits of uncommon isolation, rare glimpses of an almost forgotten island, and a spectacular ride on Ireland's only cable car.

Optional Maps: O.S. Discovery Series Map #84; also the *Beara Way Map Guide* (1:50,000) covering the entire trail which rings the Beara Peninsula; it is available at many local stores and tourist offices and from Cork Kerry Tourism (021)273251

Time/Distance: 3 hours/8.5 miles (13.6 kilometers) for the entire circuit; however, you may shorten this walk as necessary to suit your schedule.

Difficulties: Some moderate climbing; bring rain gear; there is no shelter unless you jump in one of the abandoned autos, or if the cable car is docked at the island.

Toilet Facilities: None; lots of privacy

Refreshments: None

Getting There: The cable car departs from the tip of the Beara Peninsula at Ballaghboy. It runs from 9 a.m. to 10:45 a.m., 2:30 p.m. to 5:00 p.m., and 7 p.m. to 8 p.m. The cable-car operator generally sits in a car waiting for business, and when you are ready to return you must wave for his attention. If you plan to complete the entire island tour, arrive at 10:45 and take the cable car back at 2:30 p.m. Hopefully, the cable-car operator doesn't forget your presence. Information can be obtained at (027)73017. No buses pass in this direction, and hitchers will find little traffic.

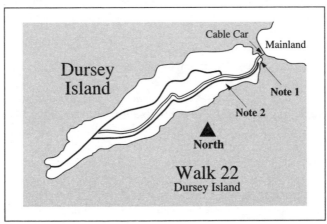

Trail Notes

___ 1. Departing from the cable car, you will notice a sign post directing you along the gravel road.

___ 2. At a crossroads, signs point in both directions. You may go in either direction and return by the opposite road when you reach the crossroads at the other end of the island.

Suggestions for More Walking

You can walk out as far as you want and return at your leisure. Also consider Walks 23 and 24 which are along the Beara Way.

Walk 23: Bere Island

Walk: Across the Island—from Ferry to Ferry via the Beara Way

80 minutes
3.7 miles (5.9 km)

General Description

Castletownbere, the largest population center on the Beara Peninsula but still diminutive, is essentially a fishing village that has begun to attract tourists who are looking for a genuine Irish experience. The bustling port lining an enormous harbor is home to a generally fishy ambiance—fishermen, fishing boats, and fish stories abound. The town exudes genuine Irish atmosphere, and most of the people in your way are locals. Stroll about the shop-lined streets, quaff Guinness copiously in dark pubs, and wander around the outdoor market. When you have imbibed enough Irish ambiance, head over to the docks for a quick cruise to Bere Island.

The short nautical excursion provides excellent views of both Bere Island and the mainland coast. Castletownbere is particularly well showcased as it unfurls at great length along the coast, looking much

larger from a distance than it did while on shore. Disembarkation signals the beginning of an intimate glimpse into the obscure, as you trek across an island seldom trodden by tourists. The already slow pace on the mainland grinds to a veritable halt here on the island. Drivers park their vehicles in the middle of the road to gossip with neighbors, secure in the realization that it could be hours before another vehicle happens along; handypeople putter endlessly in their yards; workmen stand about mutely examining the occasional pothole while contemplating the horror of future labors; normally, however, absolutely nothing at all occurs. If this sounds like paradise, several B&Bs dot the island and promise a getaway from your getaway in Ireland.

A walk across the island yields uniformly excellent views of the mainland and proximity to a variety of ancient stone homes that are being abandoned in favor of comfortable new homes. The old homes, neglected, are decaying in the harsh climate but press on picturesquely. Also decaying is the mini-armada of well placed sunken ships that are visible along the way and in the harbor at Rerrin.

Bere Island's only settlement, tidy Rerrin, sits comfortably around its tiny cove far from twentieth-century woes, except for, perhaps, poor television reception. Take the comprehensive, all-inclusive, two-minute foot tour of the town and settle back into one of the pubs while waiting for the ferry to depart. On a nice day, you may also elect to hang around the docks while enjoying views of beautiful Beara Peninsula. If you have time, explore the sparse remains of the Victorian fort on the eastern end of the island.

Optional Maps: O.S. Discovery Series Map #84; also the *Beara Way Map Guide* (1:50,000) covering the entire trail which rings the Beara Peninsula; it is available at many local stores and tourist offices and from Cork Kerry Tourism (021) 273251

Time/Distance: 1 hour 20 minutes / 3.7 miles (5.9 kilometers)

Difficulties: None

Toilet Facilities: At Rerrin

Refreshments: Pubs, restaurants, and stores at Rerrin

Getting There: Transportation can be a problem. If you cross the island from west to east, arriving at Rerrin you will be three miles (4.8 kilometers) from Castletownbere when you reach the mainland. Buses do come by this way but probably not when you need one. You can hitch a ride back to town or walk. Otherwise, take a taxi to the Murphy's dock and walk over to the western end of the island where the ferry will deliver you to Castletownbere. From Castletownbere, Bere Island Ferry (tel. 75009) runs six ferries daily to the western end of the island where this walk's description begins. You can take Murphy's Ferry Service to Rerrin (4 per day, tel. 75004). In either direction, the walk is easy to follow, but it is a good idea to bring one of the maps mentioned above.

Trail Notes

___ 1. From the dock walk directly up the only road.
___ 2. Turn left when you reach an intersection. You will see a Beara Way sign post. From this point continue along this road until you reach Rerrin. (If you are in no hurry, a right turn will take you on a tour of the island's western end.)

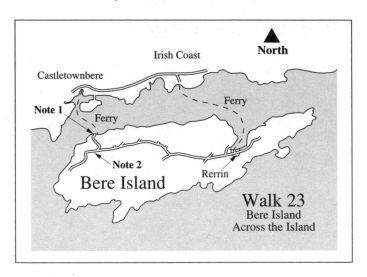

Suggestions for More Walking

It is easy to spend a day on Bere Island wandering about with the aid of the maps mentioned above which delineate all of the minor roads and trails on the island, including all of the variations of the Beara Way. Also, consider Walks 22 and 24 which are along the Beara Way. Upon return from Rerrin, you can also join up with the mainland portion of the Beara Way and follow it into Castletownbere via a mountainous path that makes for an interesting circular route.

Walk 24: Beara Village Walk

Walk: Ardgroom to Eyeries

> 180 minutes
> 7.2 miles (11.5 km)

General Description

From mountain crest to serried coast, this walk is superb in all aspects—one of the best walks anywhere in Europe. Trekking between the Beara Peninsula's most literally color-ful towns, you will greeted by one astonishing vista after another and near psychedelic town experiences at either end. Iridescent Eyeries, your destination, should receive the multi-hued facade-of-the-year award—facade colors in order of appearance (the formal arrangement of the color spectrum seems to have no import): lime green, sea green, deep blue, pale blue, light purple, bright orange, bright yellow with purple trim, beige, fuscia, deep orange, red, light yellow, light purple, pale yellow, pea green, etc., most with wildly contrasting trim. Today's trailhead, rainbow-like Ardgroom, competes fiercely (even the church is painted in a pastel purple) but, lacking an adequate number of facades, loses by numerical default.

Ardgroom, a lovely village not noted in most tourist guides, is pri-marily an interesting visual experience. However, you will want to wander about town for a few minutes and perhaps imbibe a quick pint or stop in the curious general store for trail victuals before wan-dering into the wild green yonder.

Silence quickly engulfs as you begin the ascent from Ardgroom. Although comely hills beckon your gaze, do not forget to glance from time to time over your shoulder for excellent views of Ardgroom and its pretty purple church. Climbing crookedly to ridge top, breathtaking views become increasingly expansive. At ridge top, neck craning in all direc-tions, it is as if you can see the entire world in a single panoramic view. To your right, the deep blue Atlantic Ocean stretches to infinity while to your left, emerald hills and valleys extend elegantly to the distant hori-zon. You, the independent walker, stride tall above it all.

The lengthy, isolated high ridge imparts the feeling of pathfinding across a sort of lost plateau, as if you had just tumbled out of a 1950s propeller airplane into a lost land. Disjointed flocks of sheep wander aimlessly amid great boulders contentedly ingesting voluminous volumes of gourmet grass; big birds (not the Big Bird) glide gracefully about; and a remote farm ruin, evocative of the severity of Irish life, defies the passage of time. Who would have, could have lived in this remote mountain fast?—something to contemplate as you continue this lonely ramble. Although the ridge walk can be slow as you search for the best route between waymarks, there need be no hurry since you are navigating some of Ireland's finest scenery.

Descending gradually to the coast from the rocky ridge, you will continue to marvel at the distant views in all directions. A gently flowing river meandering carelessly, casually through the valley becomes your companion as you stride to the coast where stunning views of the ocean await. Although there is an almost abandoned beach near Eyeries, the coast, rocky and heavily strewn with seaweed, is not generally accommodating to those who enjoy a combination of swimming and walking.

Along the coast near Eyeries, the extensive ruins of a great house extend in isolated, weatherbeaten magnificence. Probably from the late-nineteenth or early-twentieth century this extensive ruin has dual, massive brick chimneys, an imposing stone facade, and a continuing measure of elegance in spite of time's ineluctable ravages. As you turtle pace about the coast, vibrantly-toned Eyeries appears merrily to your left, offering surprising views as you encircle this diminutive berg for a final approach.

A lovely terminus for a superb walk, Eyeries is a visual delight that you will not hasten to leave, even though there is not much to do. Enjoy a slow stroll about town, wander into one (or more) of the pubs, and revel in the memories of a superlative day in Ireland. A final bonus: you will not see any other tourists in unspoiled Eyeries.

Optional Maps: O.S. Discovery Series Map #84; also the *Beara Way Map Guide* (1:50,000) which covers the entire trail surrounding the Beara Peninsula; available at many local stores and tourist offices and from Cork Kerry Tourism (021)273251

Time/Distance: 3 hours / 7.2 miles (11.5 kilometers)

Difficulties: It is necessary to look carefully for waymarks along the ridge where the going can be quite slow as you look for the best route between waymarks.

Toilet Facilities: None between towns; much privacy

Refreshments: None between towns

Getting There: Bus #282 departs Castletownbere for Kenmare and Killarney passing Eyeries and Ardgroom during the summer once in the morning and once in the early evening. Schedules are available at the Castletownbere tourist office or at the Killarney bus station (tel. 34777). The bus does not enter the town; it stops along R571 at the juncture of a minor road that goes to the town center.

Trail Notes

___ 1. The bus drops you at Ardgroom town center and makes a sharp right turn as it continues along R571 (there is a gas station/store at this intersection). You continue straight ahead, perpendicular to the route of the bus. You will see a Beara Way sign. Continue to follow the signs up the road as it curves around.

___ 2. Watch for the marker that takes you away from the road and directly uphill. Another marker leads to the top, and you must watch for markers along the ridge top where you turn left. They are there when you need them. (There is no definitive path on the ridge top—watch your step and follow the waymarks.)

___ 3. About 45 minutes into the walk, you will reach a gravel road where you turn left (there is a waymark). A couple minutes later, you will turn right where you see a waymark. Again, watch for the waymarks. When I came by, one was knocked over and barely visible. However, you will not get lost—just make your way to the cove you see in the distance while walking parallel to the river that is to your left.

___ 4. Descending to the river, you will to follow a gravel road to Coulagh Bay.

___ 5. Turn left at the waymark when you reach the coast.

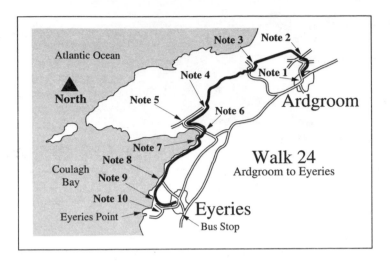

____ 6. Turn right, skirting the coast, where you see the sign indicating "Ballycrohane Stone."

____ 7. Watch for the waymark that leads up and to the left and shortly thereafter you will see another waymark to your right (this marker is easy to miss—watch carefully!).

____ 8. If you wish to shorten this walk, turn left when you reach a road that leads to a concrete dock.

____ 9. Skirting the cove, you will reach an asphalt road where you turn left and walk into Eyeries. (The official trail continues along the coast at this juncture and eventually curves around Eyeries Point and joins this road to Eyeries at the juncture in Note 10.)

____ 10. Ignore the right turn and continue straight ahead.

Suggestions for More Walking

The one possibility for shortening this walk is mentioned in note 8; it can be extended for another eight difficult miles (12.8 kilometers) by taking the bus up to Lauragh and trekking back to Eyeries. You may also wish to ponder the possibility of Lauragh to Ardgroom as another day walk. Walks 22 and 24 are also along the Beara Way.

Walk 25: A Country Ramble to the Blarney Stone

Walk: Cork to Blarney

General Description

110 minutes
5.5 miles (8.8 km)

With less than 150,000 inhabitants, underpopulated Cork is Ireland's second most populous city. According to legend, this long enduring settlement was founded by St. Finbarr in the seventh century. In horrifying reality, it was periodically ravaged by disaster and invasion during subsequent centuries. Cork was pillaged by Vikings in the ninth century, subdued by invading Anglo-Normans during the twelfth century, almost destroyed by fire in the early seventeenth century, ravaged by Cromwell's forces also during the seventeenth century, and torched by the British in the twentieth century. There are not a lot of tourists here and perhaps the residents of Cork are satisfied to be left alone.

Located on the banks of the meandering River Lee, Cork has several refined major commercial avenues encompassed by one large rough edge—industrial Ireland. If you have been crisscrossing the mall-less north country for a while, the shops of Cork, particularly along St. Patrick's Street and at the mall along Merchant's Quay, will soothe the quavering nerves of serious shoppers. As the novelty of power shopping wears thin, you may wish to visit the most recent version of St. Finbarr's Cathedral, which was constructed in 1865, replacing several earlier cathedrals. Not far from the cathedral lies the Elizabethan Fort, which was constructed by the English during the early seventeenth century to overawe the conquered Irish. Today, you may enjoy some of the best views of Cork from the ruins' parapets. History hounds will want to zip through the exhibit of the Cork Public Museum which focuses on the history of Cork from prehistoric times, and a brief nature excursion will take you to Cork Lough, a large lake within the city that is home to a bird sanctuary. Finally, Cork's most famous attraction is St. Anne's Church which is located in the Shandon neighborhood north of the River Lee. Constructed in the eighteenth century, this Anglican bastion is known for its four clocks that dominate the sides of the great tower; never synchronized, the clocks have been nicknamed "the four-faced liar." Also impressive are the circa 1752 bells, which you can play for a small fee. Tired of touring? There are plenty of places to quaff the superb, smooth-as-silk Murphy's Irish Stout that is brewed here. It is the home-town favorite and only viable rival to formidable Guinness in Ireland, the stout swilling capital of the universe.

Passing from the historic center en route to Blarney, you will begin to appreciate the less well heeled reality of Cork and industrial Ireland. Zig-zagging through a variety of busy roads, you will traverse a generally downtrodden area of foreboding industry, budget-oriented commerce, and hovel-like homes. This is a part of Ireland rarely seen by ordinary tourists and definitely off-the-beaten-path. The further from the center you progress, the more suburban the setting becomes until Upper Fair Hill Road eventually becomes a country lane. When you reach Commons Road the scenery becomes increasingly rural—fertile farmland, hills, the occasional house, and excellent views. This is a very pleasant jaunt that winds along seldom driven country lanes, (except for the last thirty minutes which requires walking along a generally safe but busy road) but in reality, you could drive this same route. I enjoyed the slow transition from urban to rural to small town and felt it was worth the time, but if you are in a hurry, drive up to Blarney along this same route.

Overcrowded Blarney is invaded on a daily basis by scores of tour buses hauling hordes of the highly feared Dreaded Other People who stand in long lines for the opportunity to osculate the Blarney Stone, an unsanitary block of limestone purported to endow the kisser with eloquent speech. I didn't stand in line for this privilege and do not feel less blessed or eloquent. You may wish to partake in this time-honored tradition; but if not, fifteenth-century Blarney Castle and its surrounding gardens are worth a quick tour. A quick stroll through the proximate Rock Close is also tranquilly engaging; here you will enjoy the nineteenth century gardens situated on a former Druid site and along the banks of the Blarney River. The most popular attraction at Rock Close is the Wishing Stairs which are supposed to be negotiated up and down with eyes closed. Hoping to walk another day, I walked up and down with my eyes aggressively open and made no wishes that would not be granted. Blarney's other main attraction is the lucrative Blarney Woolen Mills where you can buy countless high-quality sweaters and other popular tourist fare while rubbing shoulders with the stone kissers. Although I may sound a bit cynical about the Blarney experience, I actually enjoyed being here for a frantically paced mini-sojourn, enjoying both the sights and the town of Blarney where you can stroll into a variety of commodious shops, pubs, and restaurants.

Optional Maps: O.S. District Map of Cork (1:63,360) or O.S. Map #221 (1:26,720); a city map of Cork is also quite useful for navigation along city roads.

Time/Distance: 1 hour 50 minutes / 5.5 miles (8.8 kilometers)

Difficulties: About 30 minutes of annoying traffic near the end of the trail as you approach Blarney—caution is advised.

Toilet Facilities: None between towns; occasional privacy

Refreshments: Numerous opportunities in both towns

Getting There: This walk begins at Shandon Street between North Mall and Pope's Quay, which is on the north bank of the River Lee in downtown Cork where North Main Street bridges the river. If you have a car, leave it in Blarney and take one of the frequent buses from the town center to Cork.

Trail Notes

___ 1. Walk away from the River Lee on Shandon Street.

___ 2. Turn left when you reach Cathedral Street.

___ 3. Take the first right onto Wolfe Tone Street, which you will continue to follow as it becomes Fair Hill Road and Upper Fair Hill Road.

___ 4. Upper Fair Hill Road dead ends at a Telecom Eireann building where you will turn right and then quickly turn left in order to rejoin Upper Fair Hill Road.

___ 5. Arriving at a junction with a white road sign that indicates "Blarney" you will turn left onto Commons Road (R617) which is not marked at this point.

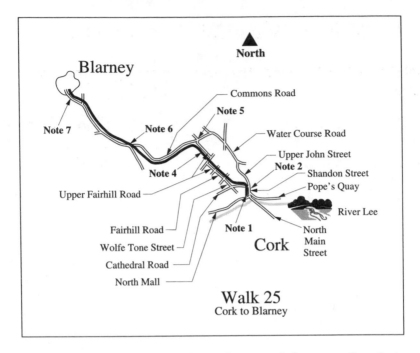

North

Blarney

Commons Road

Note 5

Note 7

Note 6

Water Course Road

Upper John Street

Note 2

Note 4

Shandon Street

Pope's Quay

Upper Fairhill Road

River Lee

Fairhill Road

Note 1

North

Wolfe Tone Street

Cork

Main

Street

Cathedral Road

North Mall

Walk 25
Cork to Blarney

____6. Commons Road deadends at a busy road that goes directly into Blarney. Turn right here. Although there is usually sidewalk or safe shoulder, be careful for 30 minutes as you make your way into Blarney.

____7. Just before you enter Blarney, watch for a wooden gate where you enter a passage made for walkers. When you come to the end of this passage there is a sign showing the direction to Blarney Castle.

Suggestions for More Walking

There are no official trails in this area that I could find. In fact, it took me some time to put together the walk described above; however, since most tourists will not want to miss Blarney and Cork it would be a disservice to not offer some sort of walk. I wish I could have found more opportunities; but, alas, this is not an area that has been developed for walkers.

Walk 26: Waterford, the Crystal Palace

Walk: A Walk along Tramore Beach

Optional time & distance

General Description

World-class Waterford crystal will delight most travelers who visit this attractively located port town on the River Suir. In fact, the Waterford Crystal factory is Waterford's primary attraction. Established in 1783, it is claimed to be the largest glassworks in the world. A fast-paced, 45 minute tour will take you from molten glass to gleaming final product. After the tour you are welcome to browse the showroom which hosts the most luminous display of crystal in the universe. From trinket sized items to monumental masterpieces, there is something for most budgets. However, the prices seem to be about the same throughout Ireland (but much cheaper than in the U.S. or elsewhere in Europe) so you do not have to wait for the Waterford Factory to buy crystal if you see something you like. On the other hand, there are many items here that you will not find anywhere else in Ireland.

Elsewhere in Waterford, there are several sights that merit inspection. In particular, you will wish to examine the walls (originally constructed by Vikings and later rebuilt by Normans) that bear mute testimony to Waterford's popularity not only with tourists but also invaders. The most impressive remnant of the ramparts is the eleventh century Reginald's Tower, which was constructed by the Vikings. Located along the Quay, this impressive monument houses the petite city museum and offers excellent views for those who wind their way to the top on the narrow staircase. As you stroll about the town, stop at Christ Church Cathedral, which was constructed in the late eighteenth century. Most interesting is the model of the original Viking church, which stood on this site from 1050 until the construction of the present edifice. Also worthy of a visit is the French Church, which was constructed by Franciscan friars in the early thirteenth century and expanded during subsequent centuries.

There are no walks that terminate at Waterford, so I decided to head south to popular Tramore with its expansive beach for a sandy strand stroll. Tramore's three-mile (5-kilometer) beach is one of Ireland's finest and most popular. Of course, this remote, cloud-encapsuled nation is not known for its beaches, and you will not mistake Tramore for St. Tropez. You will, however, enjoy outstanding views of the ocean while auscultating a stimulating symphony of crashing waves. In the distance, a friendly checkerboard pattern of forest and field encircling the entire cove greets the beachcomber/walker. Walk out as far as you wish for several memorable miles.

Tramore, attractively situated along its broad beach and climbing precipitously up high hills, is a very busy town, and most of the action unfurls along the beachside promenade where there are a variety of amusements and fast-food feeding opportunities. The town is also characterized by a variety of worlds such as Celtworld, a tacky, allegedly educational experience that dramatizes several Irish folktales—highly recommended for children and slower adults. Also suitable for family fun are nearby Splashworld featuring a wave pool and waterslides and Laserworld which allows you to simulate the murder of less favored family members in a clean, safe, and friendly environment.

Also worthy of exploration is jovial fishing village Dunmore East, the most attractive town in the Waterford area and a great place to eat and sleep. Located about ten miles (16 kilometers) south of Waterford, this diminutive municipality meanders picturesquely around a jagged cove and harbors some of Ireland's finest thatched roofs.

Optional Maps: No map is required and nothing useful is available. However, O.S. Map #23 (1:126,720) Wexford displays, with little detail, this area.

Time/Distance: Optional, up to six miles (9.6 kilometers) round trip

Difficulties: None

Toilet Facilities: None on the beach but many in town

Refreshments: Numerous pubs, restaurants, and stores in Tramore

Getting There: Tramore is eight miles (12.8 kilometers) directly south of

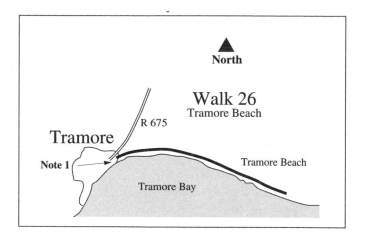

Waterford on T63. Bus Eireann also rolls frequently between Waterford and Tramore.

Trail Notes

___ 1. From Tramore, walk along the beach which extends for three miles until you decide to turn back.

Suggestions for More Walking

There is also a short cliff walk which begins at the east end of town. The map at the tourist office is helpful for a starting point. You may also wish to consider Walk 27, which is not too far from Waterford.

Walk 27: Along the River Barrow

Walk: Borris to Graiguenamanagh
via the South Leinster Way

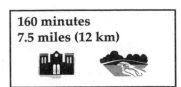

160 minutes
7.5 miles (12 km)

General Description

Borris, a one-long-street (perhaps a one-dog) town, is quite attractively situated on a gently rising hill. This results in great views but slightly more difficult trekking. Cute cottages, squeaky clean shops, inviting pubs, and enticing B&Bs line both sides of the Borris monostreet. Although there is not much to do here, you will want to stroll through the street on the way to the trail and perhaps be seduced through the threshold of a picturesque pub.

Descending to the River Barrow's well-groomed towpath, you will depart the clamor of a world increasingly dependent upon high-decible vehicular traffic and begin your time travels, luxuriating in the much slower pace of the nineteenth century when canals were a serene, silent and slow mode of transport. Striding along the towpath, try to imagine the passenger barges towed by galloping horses that regularly plied this stretch of the canal.

The canal runs along the floor of a great, green almost-primordial valley, and only the occasional farmhouse hanging from the slopes in the distance is reminiscent of encroaching civilization. The towpath paralleling the canal is quite easy to negotiate throughout its entire length; however, in some short segments the trees grow almost to the banks, forming what would be a pathless wilderness were it not for the path. To your right, the canal's waters ebb indolently but tenaciously while on the left the luxuriant blanket of sparkling wild flowers and dense shrubbery creeps to water's edge; overhead drift the ubiquitous songs of shiny, happy birds who intermingle with amiable butterflies flitting about to and fro.

Here and there ripple-forming rushes are beginning to congest the canal while water lillies, some in full bloom, wait patiently for the occasional rotund, green frog. Solitary boats drift lazily along the canal while the odd fisherman casts serenely into the river at regular intervals. Occasionally, you will spy some not-too-rapid rapids where the canal flows into the river—the roughly parallel strands of water form an interesting fast/slow or perhaps slow/slower contrast. The locks still function, and as you approach Graiguenamanagh a surprisingly inhabited lock house stands tall against the ravages of time. The luck of the Irish is certainly affirmed by the fortunate Irish person who resides here in blissful seclusion. However, the following three lock houses shrink, violet-like, in lonely abandonment having been unable to withstand time's inexorable march. After negotiating an ultra-sharp bend, your destination appears in a raiment of almost sublime simplicity—gray remoteness snugly enshrouded within a timeless emerald glen.

Graiguenamanagh, a tiny patch of isolated urbanity where farm vehicles lumber regularly along narrow streets, is truly a lovely little town unspoiled by tourism. However, it does have all the amenities that rural Ireland so generously provides—pubs, shops, lodgings—all housed in the architecturally interesting stone structures that line the narrow streets. It is also a great place to raise children who fish, climb hills, and explore paths with carefree nonchalance. Although not far from bustling Waterford, you are far from the madding crowd.

Graiguenamanagh ("grange of the monks" in the Irish language) began its existence during the thirteenth century as Duiske Abbey. The Cistercian abbey was officially dissolved and the land seized by the English in 1536, but the town prospered and began to absorb most of the land originally occupied by the monks. Take the time to call at the visitor center and then wander about the restored abbey while contemplating the lives of the hundreds of industrious monks who bustled about the grounds hundreds of years ago. If you have not spent all your crystal budget in Waterford, visit Duiske Crystal outlet where the crystal is superb and bargain priced.

Optional Maps: The South Leinster Way Map/Guide (published by East-West Mapping) is a valuable supplement to this segment and the rest of the South Leinster Way.

Time/Distance: 2 hours 40 minutes/7.5 miles (12 kilometers)

Difficulties: None

Toilet Facilities: None between towns; but much privacy

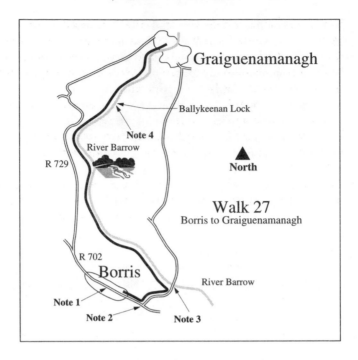

Refreshments: Pubs, restaurants, stores in both towns.

Getting There: Private buses (Foley's tel. 0503-24410 for current sched-ule) run twice per day from Graiguenamanagh to Borris, one in the early morning and one in the early afternoon. Mr. Cleary (tel. 0503-24706) is the local cab driver who can quickly and economically trans-port you at other times. It is best to reserve ahead since there is no fleet of brilliantly shined Checker Cabs at your disposal. However, since Mr. Cleary's major source of income is inebriated pub flies in need of night transport after intense imbibing, he may be available for spur-of-the-moment-impromptu travel.

Trail Notes

___ 1. The bus drops you at Dalton's Pub in Borris (if you are in a hurry, it is also possible to skip Borris and about a mile/1.6 kilometers of walking by riding the bus through town to the junction with R705—there is a sign indicating "Graiguenamanagh" to the left at this junction). From Borris walk along the road in the direction that the bus is continuing

___ 2. When you reach R705, (there is a sign indicating "Graiguenamanagh") turn left.

___ 3. When you reach the River Barrow, turn left and down on the near side to the bank. You will see a "South Leinster Way" sign at this point.

___ 4. After the fourth (Ballykeenan) lock continue on the increasingly narrow towpath, ignoring the gravel path to your left. After this point, just continue to follow the towpath into Graiguenamanagh.

Suggestions for More Walking

There is no possibility of extending or shortening this walk using public transportation. However, using Mr. Cleary's taxi service, you could take the ten-mile (16-kilometer) field and forest trek from Inistioge back to Graiguenamanagh. Also, note Walk 26, which is close to Waterford.

Walk 28: Glendalough: Grandeur in Ruin

Walk: Annamoe to Glendalough via the Wicklow Way

130 minutes
5.7 miles (9.1 km)

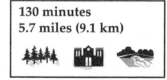

General Description

Today's superb trek to one of Ireland's most impressive historical attractions begins at Annamoe, a somnolent but appealing collection of cottages combined with a few commercial endeavors; however, beyond an interesting antique shop, you will find little to delay your departure. Trekking vertically from the valley, you will begin a gentle climb through the ancient, stone-fenced farmland that almost

envelopes the town. In the distance, your eyes will be drawn to the lovely pine-covered Wicklow Mountains, which extend ad infinitum into the horizon. The land here is rolling, alluring, extremely pacific, and beyond the ubiquitous, enthusiatically grazing sheep who shed wool everywhere, you will have this enchanted landscape to yourself.

After a great climb to a lofty hilltop, you will tread through a lovely, fragrant forest of sheltering coniferous trees. Having trod through the forest, you will begin the descent into lively lilliputian Laragh, and enjoy excellent views of the valley. The final walk into Laragh via the backdoor takes you through a dense, fragrant coniferous forest where millions of pine needles cushion your every step; you will also traverse a tiny footbridge that spans an effervescent, rapidly flowing stream.

Diminutive Laragh, situated in a deep, green valley is enveloped, almost engulfed, by a thick blanket of ineluctably expanding foliage. Close to Glendalough, you may wish to break briefly for a beverage and rub shoulders with the numerous DROPS that you have not seen since Annamoe. There are several attractive alternatives for a beverage and perhaps a snack. There is also an expensive hotel and numerous B&Bs if you are seeking lodging. (Roundwood, a few miles up the road also has a number of rooms for rent.) Departure involves a quick jaunt along the main road until you reach the local woolen mill, an ancient-looking structure where the usual assortment of finely crafted Irish wool sweaters and sundry other souvenirs is available. This is also a suitable snacktime stop.

The final river walk (one of my favorite stretches anywhere) to Glendalough is archetypically Irish green. Everything—stone fences, trees, rocks—endures an all-encompassing moss. In fact, reflecting the verdant vicinage, you will also find yourself greenish in cast. You must walk quickly here in order to avoid being overtaken by aggressively adhering moss. Trekking pacifically through the dense foliage, you will enjoy quiet river views and, as you approach Glendalough, sublime views of the ruins available only to the walker.

According to tradition, Glendalough was first inhabited by the hermit St. Kevin during the sixth century. Soon, however, followers began to arrive and St. Kevin established a monastery that was the eventual home to many thousands of devoted monks until it was destroyed by the English in the late fourteenth century.

This is truly an enchanted valley situated along a splendid river and two lovely lakes (Glendalough means "valley of the two lakes"), surrounded by great, verdant, gently sloping hills on all sides. The entire area has an otherworldly mystical appearance that tends to captivate the traveler and make hasty departures difficult.

The visitor center is the best place to begin a tour of the ruins. Located on the site of the no longer extant monastery, the center offers souvenirs, advice, a film about the history of monasteries, and guided tours of the ruins. If you choose not to be guided about the ruins, you can pick up a brochure describing the site. Although extensive, what remains is only a fraction of the original site. The most impressive ruin is the 100-foot, twelfth-century Round Tower which was used to call the monks to prayer and served as a refuge when marauding Vikings came to call. Also impressive is the cathedral, which is the largest structure still partially intact and once the largest cathedral in Ireland. Although smaller, St. Kieran's Church and St. Kevin's Church still stand in various states of ruin, and the twelve-foot St. Kevin's cross is the tallest and best preserved among many crosses. Most picturesque is the cemetery, an exceptionally pleasant abode for the dead, which provides a pause for reflection on so many lost memories of the past; many of the stones (Celtic crosses here, there, and everywhere—

and tilting at all angles) are now mute, their messages slowly erased by the inexorable passage of time. A short walk from the main site and near the banks of Upper Lake, you will discover St. Kevin's Cell said to have been inhabited by the saint, and St. Kevin's Bed, a small cave which St. Kevin used as a getaway from the stress of running the abbey.

There is no finer destination for a great day of walking. For the optimum in ruin touring, take the late afternoon bus from Glendalough to Annamoe, by the time you ramble back to Glendalough, the day trippers will be gone and you will have the ruins to yourself.

Optional Maps: O.S. Map #56 Wicklow, Dublin, Kildare; *The Wicklow Way Map Guide* (published by EastWest Mapping)

Time/Distance: 2 hours 5 minutes/5.7 miles (9.1 kilometers)

Difficulties: A long but gentle climb from Annamoe and some other some other minor ups and downs

Toilet Facilities: None between towns but much privacy

Refreshments: None between towns

Getting There: Catch the early-morning or late-afternoon bus (St. Kevin's Bus Service tel. 01 281 8119) bound to Dublin from near the monastery entrance. Ask the driver to drop you at the center of Annamoe (although Annamoe is quite tiny and consists of not much more than a center), and, in case the driver is less than vigilant, be alert for the sign indicating "Annamoe."

Trail Notes

___1. From the tiny cluster of buildings that forms the town center, look for a gravel road that goes upward in approximately the same direction that the bus had arrived in Annamoe. You will stay on this road for about ⅘ of a mile (1.3 kilometers). It is not marked. Do not take the other tiny road that branches to the right.

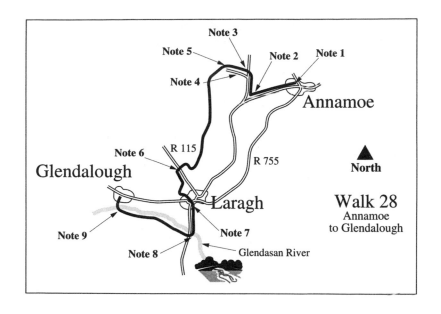

____2. In less than twenty minutes, you will dead end at an asphalt road. Turn right (you cannot get lost at this point since a left turn will take you directly into Laragh) in order to join the Wicklow Way.

____3. Turn left after about seven or eight minutes onto the first narrow gravel road (do not turn at any of the gated roads which are private drives) which is not marked, but should be since it is part of the Wicklow Way. As you ascend, there is a newer white house to your right.

____4. After another seven or eight minutes, you will reach a gate. Continue along this trail, using the style provided for your convenience.

____5. Soon, you will come to a second gate. Climb over this gate and TAKE THE TRAIL IMMEDIATELY TO YOUR LEFT. Continue to follow this trail around the forest you see ahead and you will begin to see waymarks.

____6. When you arrive at an asphalt road, turn left. Although this road goes directly to Laragh, you will turn right at a waymark away from the road in a couple of minutes.

___7. You will depart from Laragh along the main road (R755)

___8. After about seven or eight minutes on R755, you will see a sign indicating "Woolen Mill Factory Outlet Shop and Tea Room." Turn right along the gravel road that leads to this emporium. Continue along this road under the archway of the woolen mill where you will join a path that parallels the river.

___9. When you see the cemetery tower and the visitor center, watch for a bridge that will take you across the cemetery and into Glendalough.

Suggestions for More Walking

For a short version of this walk, take the bus up to Laragh and follow the trail notes beginning with #7. The length of this walk can be almost doubled by taking the bus up to Roundwood, but much of the additional mileage consists of walking along secondary roads. Long distance walkers can follow the Wicklow Way for 80 miles/128 kilometers from Dublin to Clonegal.

Dublin

Walks 29-34 are all easily completed from your base in Dublin and are designed to offer you a break from urban bustle while viewing a Dublin that few tourists have seen.

Walk 29: Along the Royal Canal in Dublin's Hinterland

Walk: Leixlip to Maynooth via the Royal Canal

70 minutes
3.8 miles (6 km)

General Description

Today you will be only about fifteen miles (24 kilometers) from Dublin but a world apart. Although no one ever stops here, Leixlip is a very busy little town in its own right with increasing numbers of citizens who commute to Dublin via numerous daily trains and buses. Beyond an attractive setting along the River Liffey and a thriving commercial sector, there is not much to do here, which is why the walk starts at the train station just beyond town—a good place for the urban weary who wish to escape Dublin for a while to begin a lonely walk. If you wish to visit Leixlip exit the train at the Leixlip Confey Station and walk into town. From town, you can walk back to Confey Station and join the canal towpath there or walk out to the Louisa Bridge Station.

Canals are delightful places that link the present to the past, and today you will trek to Maynooth via a pleasant canal towpath where you will step back a couple of centuries to a time when canals and towpaths constituted a rapid and efficient form of transportation. Unfortunately, you will be occasionally drawn back into the twentieth century by the sound of vehicular traffic (which can be disconcerting during the middle portion of the walk), even though the road is seldom visible from the trail, and there are few visual clues indicating that you are in the twentieth century.

In spite of the less than optimal aural conditions, the towpath provides a very attractive park-like atmosphere—waterlillies and wild flowers bloom; dense foliage encroaches (but everywhere the path remains negotiable); fishermen escaping family responsibilities while away hours ad infinitum; and, as a bonus, you will probably see and hear a couple of trains rumble by intent on some far off destination. Crossing under the 1795 Deey Bridge (reputed as haunted by boatmen who refused to moor here for the night—whistle in the dark as you swiftly pass) will help you put into perspective the age of the canal towpath that you are traversing. You will also pass an interesting lock house that appears to be inhabited (perhaps by ghosts) and spend some time peering into the canal at the multi-depth, green, undulating plant life that creates an emerald lava-lamp-type effect at various places along the river.

You will know that your approach to Maynooth is almost complete when the church spire inspiringly appears over the canal; and, like most towns, Maynooth appears so much grander when you approach it with great satisfaction on foot. However, having been sheltered from the DROPS along the towpath you will be shocked back into the twentieth century by Maynooth's bustling atmosphere. After quickly readjusting to the twentieth century, you will probably wish to stop for lunch or a snack at this full-service town where there are a variety of pubs and restaurants.

Maynooth Castle, constructed during the twelfth century, is Maynooth's most popular (almost its only) tourist attraction. It stands picturesquely in ruins along the main street awaiting your visitation, but a key is necessary to explore the castle grounds (relevant information is posted on the fence: present yourself at 9 Parson Street near the castle). If you do not like formalities, the fence is low and easily surmounted. The castle is in deep decline, but some towers still stand and the shady grounds are quite attractive and well maintained. St. Patrick's College, adjacent to the castle, is also worth an inspection. The visitor's center conducts tours of the venerable structures which are surrounded by alluring gardens. Established in 1795 by England's King George III, St. Patrick's was originally the only Catholic seminary in Ireland. Protestant George was reluctant to open such a subversive institution but feared that priests trained abroad may come back with even more revolutionary ideas. During the nineteenth century it was the only such institution in Ireland; today it continues a long tradition of educating for the priesthood, but in this overwhelmingly Catholic nation it is only one of many seminaries. When your tour is over, walk back to the train station for the thirty-minute ride back to Dublin. This is an interesting excursion into Dublin's hinterland that will not take much time from your sojourn in the big city.

Optional Maps: O.S. Map (1:50,000) #50 Dublin, Kildare, Meath, Wicklow; also, the spiral-bound *Guide to the Royal Canal* published by the Office of Public Works. Written for boaters, it provides detailed maps of the towpath and interesting historical commentary.

Time/Distance: 1 hour 10 minutes / 3.8 miles (6 kilometers)

Difficulties: None

Toilet Facilities: None between towns; some privacy

Refreshments: None between towns

Getting There: Both train and bus will transport you to the starting point. Bus #66 (numerous departures) from Middle Abbey St. in Dublin passes through both towns. If you are using public transportation from Dublin, take the bus up to the Louisa Bridge Station just beyond Leixlip (the station is difficult to see from the road, so ask the bus driver to call it out for you). Trains depart from Dublin's Connolly Station (14 per day). Exit at the Louisa Bridge Station. From Maynooth take the bus or train back to Dublin. By automobile, drive from Dublin to Maynooth, and take the bus (ask the bus driver to inform you when to get off), or take the train back to the Louisa Bridge Station. If public transportation does not suit your schedule, Jimmy's Taxis is almost next to the local castle.

Trail Notes

___ 1. If you have taken the bus, walk across the bridge in the direction of Maynooth; you will then descend to your left onto the tow-

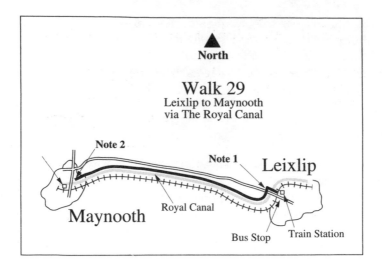

path that goes under the bridge and walk in the direction of Maynooth (do not walk back under the bridge in the direction of the train station). If you have taken the train, you will have to walk up to the bridge and follow the above directions.

___ 2. When you arrive at Maynooth, go up to the road at the first bridge. If you parked at the train station go to the left. The station is only a few yards down the road. Otherwise go right on this road (R406) which takes you to the town center at Maynooth.

Suggestions for More Walking

You can expand this walk about one mile (1.6 kilometers) by taking the bus or train to the Cope Bridge station on the north side of Leixlip. For long-distance walkers, it is possible to walk back to Dublin along the canal from either Leixlip or Maynooth. It is possible to shorten this walk by taking the bus out any point where you can access the canal. Also see the other walks in the Dublin area.

Walk 30: Dublin via the Royal Canal

Walk: Castleknock Station to Downtown Dublin

120 minutes
6.2 miles (10 km)

General Description

The Royal Canal, constructed during the late eighteenth century, links Dublin with the River Shannon about 90 miles (144 kilometers) away. Today you will traverse the canal towpath's final few miles into Dublin and experience Ireland's capital city as a Dubliner rather than a tourist. Starting from the far reaches of exurbia, you will ramble through the good, bad, and ugly that great cities conceal from all but the most cognizant travelers.

There is not much to see at Castleknock Station, today's point of embarkation, a virtual no man's land, except for a few new homes built near the tracks for Dublin commuters. After a quick trek along the tracks, you will depart the station, descend to the canal towpath, and soon be gracefully transported into a bygone era, feeling as though the twentieth century has lost its iron grip. However, you will soon be jolted back to reality by the M50 superhighway's cloverleaf junction that passes over and beneath your shocked countenance—the twentieth century's grip is not so easily broken, even along an eighteenth-century canal. This is a walk of many contrasts.

Beyond M50, you will begin what is essentially a rural trek through a major metropolis. Nowhere in the middle of somewhere is an apt description—road sounds in the distance are often your only link to modernity. Along the way, you will stride beneath still-functioning, eighteenth-century bridges that represent an excellent value for the Irish taxpayer's investment; be dazzled by frequent stands of wild flowers along the often heavily treed banks; spy rabbits that appear briefly before scurrying back into the bushes (not desirous of becoming dinner for some insensitive rambler); savor the suavely sophisticated swans that float regally along the canal; and peer into the waters which are becoming choked by plant life (although still navigable) and needs to be dredged. Continuing along, you will reach the first lock house which is inhabited and held hostage by an aggressive Irish garden. The owner is ensured rural tranquility within minutes of Dublin's huddled masses and could possibly swim to work or perhaps hire a small launch. In any case, this is a highly desirable property. Passing the lock house, Ireland's largest city remains far from mind, but the mysterious red and orange lights that are confronted here and there may perplex the bewildered walker. Do not stop or hesitate at a red light; hope, however, that the trains obey the signals.

Not far after the Ashtown station, suburban and rural begin to interwine as subdivisions abruptly appear as if recently willed by some higher being. However, the towpath retains its bucolic nature, and if you march lockstep, head pointed directly forward, the new houses are not noticeable. After Reilly's Bridge foreboding factories and warehouses, uninvitingly encased in voluminous reels of razor wire, rise regularly from the boundaries of the canal, indicating the increasingly urban nature of the walk. Some factories appear more heavily fortified than a staunchly defended medieval fortress.

That canals were in fact commercial and industrial byways is most clear on this walk. Political and other graffiti is scrawled on any available concrete—"FREE ALL POLITICAL PRISONERS," "MICKEY, CHARLIE, ETC." were here, "MORO LOVES SUZ," and the like ad nauseum. Closer to Dublin, more pedestrians are encountered, most of them participating in local transhumance, passing from house to house on this pedestrian superhighway.

By the time you reach the Broome Bridge Station, the sights and sounds of industrial Ireland are exploding in earnest—in cutting contradiction to the natural beauty theme that has been pervasive along other walks throughout Ireland. However, even after the Broome Bridge Station, there are occasional patches of rural tranquility.

Reaching Cross Guns Bridge, the Dublin cacophony surges into increasingly higher decibels, but along the canal, a certain peace reigns tenuously. Even as you approach the heart of Dublin along this florid path which skirts the homes of Dubliners (you will be able to peer into their backyards) the canal provides a relaxing respite from urban unease. No other guidebook will take you on a walk like this, into the heart of the real Dublin through the real back door.

Optional Maps: O.S. Map #50 (1:50,000) clearly shows the route but does not provide much urban detail. Any Dublin map that extends out to M50 will also be useful. Also, a Dublin map is necessary to help you navigate at walk's end. Finally, the spiral-bound *Guide to the Royal Canal*, published by the Office of Public Works and written for boaters, provides detailed maps of the towpath and interesting historical commentary.

Time/Distance: 2 hours / 6.2 miles (10 kilometers)

Difficulties: BRING A CITY MAP OF DUBLIN TO HELP YOU NAVIGATE THE URBAN LABYRINTH AT WALK'S END. Also, you may wish to abandon the walk at Drumcondra Road where the towpath becomes more menacing and lonely (see note 3).

Toilet Facilities: None, but some privacy.

Refreshments: Stores at Cross Guns Bridge; otherwise, you must wait until you begin to see stores and pubs after leaving the towpath

Getting There: From Connolly Station in Dublin's center, take the train out to Castleknock Station.

Trail Notes

____ 1. When you arrive at the Castleknock Station, walk back in the direction of Dublin to the bridge you see. Cross over the bridge to the other side. Having crossed the bridge, you will see the towpath where you will turn right in the direction of Dublin.

____ 2. At the Ashtown station go left across the tiny bridge over the canal and continue in the direction of Dublin.

____ 3. At Drumcondra Road you must cross by the light if you decide to continue along the towpath. However, the path at this point becomes quite urban in the most negative sense of the word, and you may wish to turn right at this point along Drumcondra Road which becomes Upper Dorset Street. A couple of blocks later, you will turn left on North Circular Road which you will follow up to Amiens Street where you will turn right and soon arrive at Connolly Station.

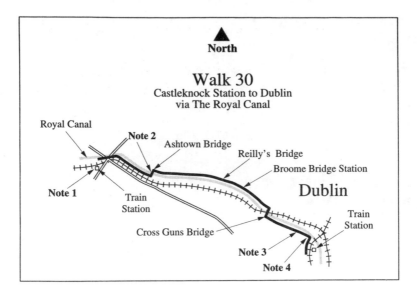

▲
North

Walk 30
Castleknock Station to Dublin
via The Royal Canal

Royal Canal

Note 2

Ashtown Bridge

Reilly's Bridge

Broome Bridge Station

Note 1

Dublin

Train
Station

Train
Station

Cross Guns Bridge

Note 3

Note 4

___ 4. If you choose to continue along the towpath, turn right at North Strand Road which soon becomes Amiens Street and takes you to Connally Station.

Suggestions for More Walking

You can shorten or lengthen this walk by taking the train to the station of your choice. Look on the O.S. Map #50 which shows all the stations as red dots up to Maynooth. Also consider the other Dublin walks covered in this book.

Walk 31: Dublin via the Grand Canal

Walk: Clondalkin to Downtown Dublin

120 minutes
6 miles (9.6 km)

General Description

This is a very eventful six miles (9.6 kilometers) right into the heart of Dublin from the middle of absolutely nowhere. You will descend from the train at Clondalkin, a nondescript industrial/commercial area that is nowhere near the beaten tourist track. Do not tarry long, but stride immediately to the Grand Canal. Constructed during the late nineteenth century, this venerable waterway links Dublin with the River Shannon. It is interesting to imagine what the Grand Canal was like 200 years ago when this was one of the two major transportation links to Dublin, and I suspect that it was quite disorderly at times. As you pass the Eighth Lock (the first lock encountered on the way to Dublin from Clondalkin), ponder the Christmas Eve sinking of a passenger barge with the loss of eleven lives. The tragic accident was attributed to the riotous behavior of the passengers.

Not far from Clondalkin, as you pass beneath the colossal M50 interchange, the walk begins to display the characteristics of urban sprawl increasingly found in Europe's major cities. Often you will see Dublin at its least attractive along this somewhat disturbing trek that stands in pointed contradiction to the usual bucolic serenity encountered in Ireland. With cyclopean electrical towers looming overhead, you will pass an attractively appointed junkyard; survey makeshift dumps here and there; and puzzle over unsightly warehouses girdled by aesthetically arranged coiled steel and barbed wire as protection from urban marauders.

Children (who I suspect have short life expectancies) swim recklessly in the murky waters; non-threatening, mangy dogs dart about here and there; horses graze lazily along overgrown banks while curious menageries forage on the grounds of large manufacturing complexes. Meanwhile, row upon row of newly erected townhouses threaten to engulf the narrow walkway; occasional fishermen gripped by disturbing catatonia dip their lines into the dark waters (I wonder what toxins lie within their catch); and wherever there is a bridge, there is graffiti.

The canal itself is in need of a good dredging—thick vegetation encroaches, resulting in a difficult-to-negotiate waterway. Even though few admirers pass, it also makes an attractive haven for city-weary swans; and, when you avert your eyes from the shadowy waters, you will see the Wicklow Mountains to the south which at times appear close enough to touch.

The canal towpath becomes more genteel by the time you reach Tyrconnell Road—people walk their dogs, sit stoically on benches, jog great distances, and socialize extemporaneously with familiar faces. However, this span is not totally genteel since I did notice that some third-floor apartment balconies are totally barred in an attempt to ward off determined intruders.

Leaving the canal, you will begin to traverse the people's Dublin and course along streets that harbor rows of townhouses and apartment buildings punctuated by diminutive shops and local restaurants. You will also pass the Guinness brewery on James Street where you may stop for a tour, souvenirs, and a refreshing drink straight from the source. Approaching Trinity College, you will be in the heart of historic Dublin, and shoulder to shoulder with less adventurous tourists, you can be certain that no one else has been where you have been. You have experienced a fascinating six-mile transition which illustrates that in European cities (in distinct contrast to American cities) wealth is still concentrated at the city center while the impecunious are relegated to the fringes or hidden beyond the pale.

Optional Maps: O.S. Map #50 (1:50,000) clearly shows the route but does not provide much urban detail. Any Dublin map that extends out to M50 will also be useful. Also, a Dublin map is necessary to help you navigate at walk's end. Finally, the spiral-bound *Guide to the Grand Canal*, published by the Office of Public Works and written for boaters, provides detailed maps of the towpath and interesting historical commentary.

Time/Distance: 2 hours / 6 miles (9.6 kilometers)

Difficulties: None

Toilet Facilities: None until downtown Dublin; some privacy

Refreshments: Numerous stores, restaurants, bars, and cafes as you leave the canal and walk through the heart of Dublin.

Getting There: Trains to Clondalkin depart frequently from Heuston Station (be certain to get on the correct train; the super-long, sleek ones do not stop at Clondalkin; if in doubt, ask). From Connolly Station, buses run frequently to Heuston Station on the other side of the River Liffey.

Trail Notes

____ 1. Emerging from the train at the Clondalkin Station, you will walk back in the direction of Dublin towards the stairway (do not use the stairs) that leads over the tracks. You will soon pass through a gate and ascend to the road where you will go right (either of the two roads that run perpendicular to the tracks will take you to the trail).

____ 2. In a couple minutes, when you intersect with another more heavily trafficked road, turn left.

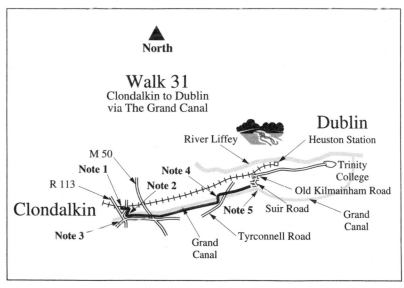

_____ 3. When you cross the canal, go left in the direction of Dublin along the towpath.

_____ 4. At Tyrconnell Road, cross to the other side of the canal.

_____ 5. When you reach the bridge at Suir Road, turn left and continue one or two blocks past South Circular Road turning right on either busy Old Kilmainham Road or less-busy Kilmainham Road (there were no street name signs when I passed this way). The roads eventually merge (after numerous name changes) and take you directly into Trinity College. At this point you can jump on a bus heading into Dublin center.

Suggestions for More Walking

When you reach the bridge and Suir Road, you could continue along the towpath, but it simply follows the road in a wide arc around the city while omitting the most interesting sights. Also, you can shorten or lengthen this walk by taking the train to a closer or more distant station. Look on the O.S. Map #50 which shows all the stations as red dots. Also consider the other Dublin walks covered in this book.

Walk 32: Dublin/Howth Peninsula

Walk: Howth to Sutton via the Howth Cliff Walk

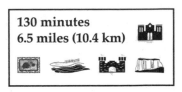

130 minutes
6.5 miles (10.4 km)

General Description

Howth lies at the end of a peninsula about ten miles (16 kilometers) north of downtown Dublin along the Dublin Bay. Easy access is assured via a thirty-minute rail ride along Dublin's rapid transit system, DART. This is a superlative destination for flight from Dublin's harried pace: a variety of accommodations are available along the calm, village-like streets, and several minor attractions may delay your cliff walk. St. Mary's Abbey, now in ruins but still partially standing, provides a glimpse into the lives of medieval monks who resided in this remote corner of Christendom. The National Transport Museum just out of town (walk along Harbour Road until you see the signs for the museum and Deer Park Hotel) houses an improbable collection of motorized and horse-drawn vehicles. Medieval Howth Castle stands restored along the way to the museum but is currently inhabited and not open for visitation. You may, however, admire the extensive gardens as you trek past. Island hoppers can visit the small isle Ireland's Eye just off the coast which is now a bird sanctuary (Frank Doyle and Sons located on the East Pier can ferry you there for a reasonable price). However, during the Middle Ages, it was home to early Christians who built a church which is now in almost total ruin. The town itself stretches along the coast and up the hill. Only 30 minutes from Dublin's harried pace, Howth (still somewhat of a fishing village) slows to a snail's pace. Here you can relax at a waterfront restaurant while enjoying the catch of the day which has been trawled from the sea only hours ago. If you are looking for a quiet environment for your sojourn in Dublin, you have found it.

The trek out of town takes you past an armada of fishing boats intermingled with pleasure craft, masts packed densely in forest-like proportions. A motley collection of near-mansions and quasi-shacks also lines the way out of town. The trail begins by overlooking a rocky, boulder stewn beach which from a sun-bather's point of view is not very inviting. Soon, however, a beach suitable for lounging comes into view. As you ramble away from town, look back—the views of Howth are outstanding.

As the trail departs the asphalt road, it becomes rocky and winding while tracing the circuitous wanderings of the coast. The sea is virtually ubiquitous with views only occasionally obscured by dense foliage. Plying the choppy waters are frequent freighters, elegant sail boats, and an occasional three-masted schooner. Farther along, one craggy promontory after another marks the trail while brilliantly effusive wild flowers cling tenuously to the steep cliffs. Crumbling, foliage covered walls appear regularly, and there are a number of opportunities to descend from the trail to sandy beaches which are generally very secluded. You will also pass powerfully situated Baily lighthouse where, I have been told, a walk down to the entrance will be rewarded by a quick look around. Near Sutton you will pass a well preserved, round defensive structure known as a martello tower which was constructed in the early nineteenth century when Ireland was anticipating a French invasion. Sutton, your destination, is an attractive village which hosts a variety of shopping, dining, and drinking opportunities. However, it is quite busy and not in the same league with Howth as a Dublin base.

Today you have enjoyed if not an end-of-the-world type of experience, at least and end-of-the-peninsula type of experience. An experience that will not soon fade from your memory.

Optional Maps/Topo-Guides: O.S. Discovery Series Map #50; many local Dublin maps include the Howth Peninsula; particularly detailed is the O.S. Map of Greater Dublin (1:20,000).

Time/Distance: 2 hours 10 minutes / 6.5 miles (10.4 kilometers)

Difficulties: None

Toilet Facilities: None between towns; some privacy

Refreshments: Restaurants, bars, and stores in both towns

Getting There: From Dublin take the DART train to the last stop north at Howth. Trains run approximately every fifteen minutes.

Trail Notes

____ 1. Turn left along the coast road as you emerge from the station, walking past the docks, the Texaco station and the St. Lawrence Hotel. Continue to follow this road until it becomes Balscadden Road and eventually becomes the trail.

____ 2. When the asphalt ends, you will see a fork in the trail; go right and up.

____ 3. When you reach a dead end you will see a large home with a gate called Gale Point. Go left and then almost immediately right at the side of the home where you see a narrow grassy path which continues along the coast.

____ 4. A couple of minutes past the turn mentioned in note 3, you will arrive at a point where you will go right and up. Do not take the

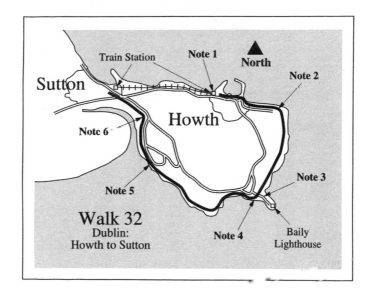

paths that lead to the lighthouse or the cliff.
___ 5 The trail ends at an asphalt road (Strand Road) where you turn left and continue to follow the coast.
___6. Strand Road dead ends at Greenfield Road where you turn left and follow this road (the name changes to Station Road) down to the DART station where you may take the train back to Dublin.

Walk 33: Dublin South

Walk: **Killiney Hill Park to Dun Laoghaire via the Dun Laoghaire Way**

| 80 minutes |
| 4.5 miles (7.2 km) |

🌲🌲 🏰 〜 🖼️

General Description

Killiney Hill Park, just south of Dublin and covering most of tall Dalkey Hill, requires a precipitous climb as soon as you descend from the bus. However, ascending to the hilltop obelisk (constructed during the mid-eighteenth century), you will be astonished by distant views of seemingly endless beaches to the south and long vistas of the sea merging mistily with remote Wales along the horizon. Soon after, you will pace through Killiney Hill Forest where the hyper-green experience is mystical—gnarled undergrowth engulfs massive boulders and moss covered crumbling stone walls while brilliant, multi-hued wild flowers blanket the forest floor. The descent will take you along beautiful stone walls and directly through an abandoned stone structure, silent for hundreds of years. Excellent views abound throughout the entire descent. Near sea level, house spotters will begin enjoying glimpses of some of the luxurious lodgings which were built for the Dublin elite early in this century.

Just off the trail (see note 7), you may visit elegant Dalkey Village (Bernard Shaw's childhood home). Haven for wealthy shoppers and well heeled diners, Dalkey is a good place to rub shoulders with the local elite while imbibing a mid-walk beverage. Although currently incorporated into Dun Laoghaire, Dalkey was previously a heavily fortified redoubt. Several fortifications still exist, including twelfth-century Bulloch Castle near the shore and Goat Castle which has been incorporated into the town hall.

Continuing along coastal Harbour Road, the sea occasionally peeks through the rows of gilded mansions, and close to Dun Laoghaire you will stride sandy beaches into the expansive docks that serve as the principal port for traffic from Great Britain. Don't miss the National Maritime Museum which is appropriately situated in the Mariners' Church and

houses a variety of nautical exhibits including a dazzling lamp from the Baily lighthouse at Howth. Literary lions will want to stop on the way in at the Sandycove martello tower (where Joyce stayed briefly in 1904) that houses the James Joyce Museum. The interesting collection includes the author's death mask, some first editions, correspondence, and a variety of personal items.

Optional Maps/Topo-Guides: O.S. Discovery Series Map #50; many local Dublin maps include this route, particularly detailed is the O.S. Map of Greater Dublin (1:20,000).

Time/Distance: 1 hour 20 minutes / 4.5 miles (7.2 kilometers)

Difficulties: A short climb to Killiney Hill

Toilet Facilities: At bars and restaurants in Dalkey and Dun Laoghaire; some privacy

Refreshments: Bars and restaurants at Dalkey and Dun Laoghaire

Getting There: From Dublin take the frequent running DART train to Dun Laoghaire and then the #59 bus from in front of the DART station to its last stop on the top of Killiney Hill (the bus turns around and returns to Dun Laoghaire at this point).

Trail Notes

___ 1. Directly across from the bus stop you will see a stone staircase that you will ascend and then continue upwards to the large stone monument, an obelisk, at the top of the hill.

___ 2. After passing the obelisk, you will come to a fork where you will go right continuing to follow the coastal path which is asphalted and staircased (do not go left and down while you are in the park).

___ 3. When you reach a stone fence on Dalkey Hill (watch for distant views of Dublin) continue to follow it as it winds around while descending

___ 4. When you arrive at a vehicular road, go left for about twenty feet and then go right at a staircase that will bring you to the coast road (Vico Road) where you go left and continue into Dun Laoghaire. You will see a sign indicating the "Dun Laoghaire Way" but no other signs were visible when I passed this way.

___ 5. At the first intersection, turn right (Sorrento Road which is not marked at this point).

___ 6. At the end of Sorrento Road, turn left on Coliemore Road.

___ 7. At Leslie Street, turn right (if you continue on Coliemore you will enter in a couple of minutes lovely downtown Dalkey). Continue along this street as it becomes Harbour Road.

___ 8. When Harbour Road dead ends at Breffni Road, turn right.

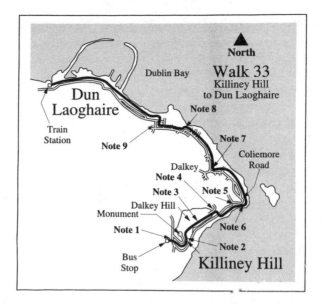

___ 9. From Harbour Road, turn right on the second road called Sea Front, and then take the first left from Sea Front to the coast road again and follow it to the DART station.

Suggestions for More Walking

You may wish to do some beach walking between the Bray station and Killiney using the DART train to get from point to point.

Walk 34: Dublin's Wicklow Way

alk: **Marlay Park to Glencullen**
a the Wicklow Way

170 minutes
7 miles (11.2 km)

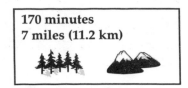

General Description

Beloved by Dubliners, Marlay Park is a captivatingly beautiful park with vast open spaces, dense forests, open air art, innumerable benches and an air of preternatural calm—a great place to lounge leisurely on a solar friendly afternoon. You will soon leave the locals behind and traverse the park path, which is heavily forested and follows a fast flowing stream. Here and there placid ponds lie quietly, visually enhancing an already pleasing stretch of the Wicklow Way.

As you leave the park along Kilmashogue Lane, enjoy the impressive homes and the startlingly distant views of Dublin (the greatest panoramas of a capital city that I have ever been privileged to view), Dublin Bay, the Howth Peninsula and beyond. Multimillion dollar views for free (or, more exactly, for the toll that is exacted by a fifteen-minute climb)—the non-walker omits the most wonderful aspects of Dublin. Continuing upward, you will skirt a mile-high golf course with incredible views over Dublin. Stronger walkers can sling clubs over their shoulder and play a few holes before continuing along the trail. Hilltop attained, you will cut through a very fragrant coniferous forest before emerging to an entirely different but equally spectacular set of views—Dublin disappears but is replaced by astonishing views of the seemingly endless Wicklow Mountains. The hilltop descent continues to astonish until valley floor is attained. After a quick road walk, you will arrive at Glencullen which is basically two golf courses and the popular Johnny Fox's Tavern. The tavern, promoted as being the highest pub in Ireland, is a great place to stop for a pint of Guinness at the end of a hot, dusty but unforgettable country ramble.

Optional Maps: O.S. Map (1:50,000) #50 shows the course of the trail and O.S. Map of Greater Dublin (1:20,000) is highly recommended since it details the streets around Marlay Park and indicates the bus routes.

Any other detailed Dublin map would also be helpful.

Time/Distance: 2 hours 50 minutes/7 miles (11.2 kilometers)

Difficulties: About fifteen minutes of hard climbing from Marlay Park and a total of about 30 minutes of other climbing. This walk does require some endurance.

Toilet Facilities: Marlay Park and Johnny Fox's Tavern at Glencullen; much privacy

Refreshments: Snacks and beverages at Marlay Park and at Glencullen

Getting There: If you have a car, drive south of Dublin to Glencullen which is located near the bottom (close to the southeast corner) of O.S. Map #50. From Glencullen (the bus stops at the side of Johnny Fox's Tavern on Ballyedmonduff Road—you will be going in the direction of Stepaside and Dublin) take bus 44B into the center of Dundrum which is the first small town after Glencullen (ask the driver to announce your arrival and watch for the church, a crossroads, numerous shops, etc.). There is a cab stand here, and you may wish to save time and confusion by availing yourself of this service. If you are continuing by bus, walk back from the bus stop near the church to the intersection where you turn left and walk a couple minutes up the hill to a bus stop. Buses run every fifteen minutes and either of the two buses will take you to the same point near Marlay Park. The bus leaves Dundrum and continues along Ballinteer Avenue until it makes a sharp right on Broadford Road where you will exit. Continue on foot along Ballinteer Avenue until you reach Grange Road which skirts the park perimeter. Turn right at Grange Road and continue along this road until you see a park entrance to your left. If you are not driving, take the bus (47, 47A, 47B, 48A, or 75 either take you to the park entrance or the general vicinity—look at your Dublin map for the exact route) to Marlay Park and, at walk's end, take bus 44B back to Dublin. Call for the schedule (tel. 873 4222 or 872 0000) since buses are not frequent from Glencullen. Alternately, you could call a taxi from the tavern at Glencullen while imbibing your favorite brew in congenial company.

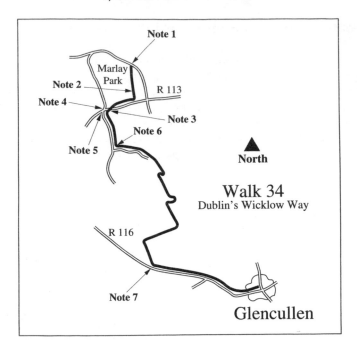

Note 1

Marlay
Park

Note 2

R 113

Note 4

Note 3

Note 6

Note 5

▲
North

Walk 34
Dublin's Wicklow Way

R 116

Note 7

Glencullen

Trail Notes

___ 1. Once in the park, begin to walk south on the forested path and watch for the brown signposts that indicate "Wicklow Way." (If you prefer, it is possible to take any route to the park's back wall where you will turn right.)

___ 2. When you reach the wall at the southern extremity of the park, turn right and continue along the trail.

___ 3. When you come to a gate, walk out of the park and to your right on College Road where you will see a trail indicator.

___ 4. Where College Road dead ends, go left on Tibradden Road.

___ 5. IMPORTANT: almost immediately, you will turn left onto Kilmashogue Lane.

___ 6. Watch for the arrow that takes you left along a narrow asphalt road. Watch carefully for the arrows at this point. You will be guided along a wide forest track and then to your right and

upwards along a rocky path just before the final des
Glencullen.

_____ 7. When you reach the road, go left and walk into Glencullen (.
after about twenty minutes of walking along the road, you
see an arrow taking you to the right; IGNORE this arrow
continue along the road to Glencullen). If you are tired, you m
try hitching a ride at this point, although there is very little tra.
fic along this road. If one of the very rare buses appears as you
begin the road walk to Glencullen, consider the possibility of
divine intervention.

Walk 35: The Great Abbey

Walk: **Clonmacnoise via the Pilgrim's Road**

Optional Time & Distance

General Description

Clonmacnoise, situated along a lovely bend of the River Shannon, rivals Glendalough in beauty of site and structures. Founded during the mid-sixth century by St. Kieran, Clonmacnoise was the culmination of the saint's mystical vision. While studying on Inishmore Island, St. Kieran had a vision of a great tree extending its branches over all Ireland. Fellow St. Enda interpreted this as a great church to be founded by Kieran along the banks of the River Shannon. From these obscure, sixth-century origins Clonmacnoise grew steadily into a massive complex of religious structures and monks' quarters. The holy site was looted during many raids over the centuries and finally abandoned during the sixteenth century. Today the oldest structures date from the ninth century.

Stop at the visitors' center for the audio-visual show, and spend a few moments inspecting a variety of venerable grave stones dating from the eighth to the twelfth century before entering the monastic site. The present-day religious complex with its numerous Celtic crosses and venerable religious structures scattered aesthetically along the

verdant banks of the River Shannon, is a magnificent sight. The cathedral is the largest extant structure and is a jumble of parts assembled beginning in the tenth century when the original wooden structure was   replaced by more durable stone. Over the centuries, the cathedral was vandalized and rebuilt a number of times with the newest parts dating back to the fifteenth century. Temples in close proximity to the cathedral include: the twelfth century Temple Doolin which was restored in the late seventeenth century for use as a mausoleum, Temple Meaghlin also from about the twelfth century, and Temple Kieran which reportedly contains the remains of the eponymous saint. Temples abound here as do the ubiquitous Celtic crosses. The nine-foot South Cross, erected during the eighth century, depicts the crucifixion and is the oldest of these crosses. The ten-foot Cross of the Scriptures, perhaps the most interesting of these impressive monuments, is embellished with a variety of Biblical scenes including the Last Judgment, and depictions of Christ's last days on earth.

Forcing yourself to pass from these mystical grounds, you will begin a trek along the Pilgrim's Way which was named for the great waves of transhumance that swept along its hallowed path during important holy days. Although this road is still used at certain times of the year by

pilgrims, none of the throngs that mill about the grounds of Clonmacr
can be detected on the Pilgrim's Road. Although this road is open to c
virtually none pass, and you will find this to be a very tranquil rou
where you may ponder the passage of time while conjuring in the mind
eye the masses of penitent pilgrims who trod this ancient route.

A few minutes after leaving the gate you will come upon the
diminutive Nun's church which was constructed in 1167 and restored
in 1865. Currently it stands lonely in near ruin, but is still evocative of
times long and forever lost. Enjoy excellent views of the river swirling
gracefully along its tangential course while boats glide quietly by. Farther along, you will walk into the most pleasant world of generic-Irish-
cow-grazing scenery where lots of lazy sheep and their fallen wool
line the way. The walk is rolling, green, and tranquil. Views of
Clonmacnoise and its towering tower are inspiring as you begin the
return walk—imagine the awe inspired in the hearts of medieval pilgrims and their satisfaction at attaining such a difficult goal.

This is an excursion well worth the drive from Dublin or Galway.
Although Clonmacnoise can be done as a long day trip, you may wish
to spend an evening at nearby Athlone, which is also worth a quick
visit. Animated Athlone straddles the banks of the River Shannon just
south of lovely Lough Ree. Its central location made it a candidate for
capital of the Irish Republic in the early twentieth century, but a near
win is no win in the world of politics—Dublin is the capital and Athlone
continues to lurk in the penumbra of national glory. The thirteenth-
century castle is Athlone's major tourist draw. Towers and walls continue to stand tall and a tour of the battlements is enhanced by the
excellent views of the town and river. There is also an audio-visual
show depicting the seventeenth-century siege of Athlone when Jacobite
forces were overwhelmed by the Williamite army. A small museum
that chronicles local history is located deep in the keep and worth a
quick look. Music lovers will delight in the souvenirs from local son
and famed tenor John McCormack's career. You may also wish to visit
the cavernous church of Saints Peter and Paul which was built during
the early twentieth century and posesses some great stained glass windows. A stroll about town is quite pleasant and may lead you into the
diminutive but high-quality Athlone Crystal factory.

~ional Maps: There are no useful maps, but it is impossible to ~come lost.

Time/Distance: You can walk as far as you wish and return along the same road.

Difficulties: Some minor ups and downs as the land begins to roll

Toilet Facilities: Public restrooms at Clonmacnoise

Refreshments: Available at Clonmacnoise

Getting There: At the end of what is called the New Cemetery, there is a gate. Pass through the gate and go to your left along the narrow asphalt road.

Trail Notes

___ 1. Continue along the Pilgrim's Road until you are ready to return along the same path.

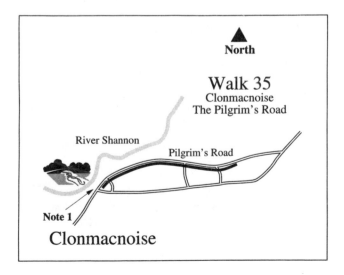